EXPRESSIONS

· ·

S T O R I E S   A N D   P O E M S

Pat Fiene
Project Editor

Karen A. Fox
Research and Development

CB

CONTEMPORARY BOOKS

a division of NTC/CONTEMPORARY PUBLISHING GROUP
Lincolnwood, Illinois USA

Library of Congress-Cataloging-in-Publication Data

Expressions : stories and poems.
       p.   cm. — (Contemporary's whole language series)
      ISBN 0-8092-3993-0 (paper)
      1. Readers (Adult)   2. Readers—1950–   I. Series.
PE1126.A4E97   1991
428.6—dc20   91-25363
                                      CIP

ISBN: 0-8092-3993-0

Published by Contemporary Books,
a division of NTC/Contemporary Publishing Group, Inc.,
4255 West Touhy Avenue,
Lincolnwood (Chicago), Illinois, 60712-1975 U.S.A.
© 1992 by NTC/Contemporary Publishing Group, Inc.
Manufactured in the United States of America

  0 1 2 3 4 5 6 7 QB(M) 23 22 21 20 19 18 17 16 15

Editorial Director
Caren Van Slyke

Assistant Editorial Director
Mark Boone

Editorial
Peter Shrock
Craig Bolt
Leah Mayes
Cliff Wirt

Editorial Assistant
Erica Pochis

Editorial Production Manager
Norma Fioretti

Production Assistant
Marina Micari

Cover Design
Georgene Sainati

Cover Illustrator
Maria Stroster

Fine Art Consultant
Steven Diamond

Typography
Terrence Alan Stone

TO THE READER

What will you find in this book? Readable, interesting stories and poems chosen with you in mind.

As you read, you will meet some entertaining and unusual people: a minor-league ballplayer waiting for a break into the majors, ex-lovers meeting by chance in New York City, and a man who spends his day giving people tickets for their bad behavior. You will read about men acting like boys, boys trying to be men, and two women trying to understand each other's language and culture.

The people appear in a variety of places—a mysterious car wash, a busy airport, an empty apartment, and a home deep in the woods. The action takes place in New York City, Vietnam, Tampa, and the Middle East.

The people may remind you of someone you know—maybe even of yourself. Though they are fictional, they seem very real. Like us, they must face and solve problems to find happiness and success.

After you read a story or poem, take time out to reflect and to write. Draw on your own experiences to understand the experiences of the people you read about. On your way to understanding them, you will come to understand more about yourself.

We hope that you enjoy *Expressions*.

The Editors

CONTENTS

BEGINNING

They Went Home   1
Maya Angelou

Early Autumn   5
Langston Hughes

The Sunday News   10
Dana Gioia

One Throw   13
W. C. Heinz

APO 96225   22
Larry Rottmann

Tickits   27
Paul Milenski

BUILDING

Collect Calls   32
Diana Bickston

Speed Cleen   35
James Stevenson

Montgomery   42
Sam Cornish

She Said a Bad Word   45
Jose Yglesias

Note to the Previous Tenants   55
John Updike

Thief   59
  Robley Wilson, Jr.

Fifteen   65
  William Stafford

North Light   69
  Mark Helprin

E X T E N D I N G

The Dream   76
  Randall Jarrell

Andrew   79
  Berry Morgan

The Telephone   88
  Edward Field

Bicycles, Muscles, Cigarettes   91
  Raymond Carver

Filling Station   105
  Elizabeth Bishop

The Lesson   109
  Toni Cade Bambara

Note to the Instructor: The teacher's guide contains a step-by-step lesson plan and activities for every story and poem.

How does it feel to love someone who doesn't feel the same way about you? As you read, think about how the woman in the poem feels. Does she think, What's wrong with me? Has she given up? Also listen to the sounds of the words, the rhythm, and the rhyme. Maya Angelou has been a singer and a dancer. Her poems are very musical.

They Went Home

Maya Angelou

They went home and told their wives,
    that never once in all their lives,
    had they known a girl like me,
But . . . They went home.

They said my house was licking clean,
    no word I spoke was ever mean,
    I had an air of mystery,
But . . . They went home.

My praises were on all men's lips,
    they liked my smile, my wit, my hips,
    they'd spend one night, or two or three.
But . . .

REFLECT ·······································

What is troubling the woman in the poem? How do you know?

What is the speaker's attitude toward men? What is her attitude toward herself?

Read the poem out loud, using your voice to show different feelings. The first time that you read the poem, make your voice sound sad; the second time, angry; the third time, sarcastic. Which of these emotions do you think the woman is feeling? How can you tell?

Which words in the poem rhyme? Which words and lines are repeated?

How do rhyming words and repetition add to the music of the poem?

WRITE ································

The woman in the poem lists some of her good points—things that people like about her. Choose one of the following beginnings, and write about one of your own good points.

- My best quality is . . .
- People like me because . . .
- The quality other people most admire in me is . . .

Imagine that you are the woman in the poem, and write a short "Dear Abby" letter telling about your problem. Then write a short letter back, telling the woman how to solve her problem. If you want, use the following beginnings to get started.

Dear Abby,   Dear Lonely,
I have a problem with   Here's what you should
the men in my life . . .   do to solve your
                            problem . . .

Should people get married, or should they stay single? Explain which you think is better, giving at least three reasons why.

William Clutz, *Morning Jogger*, 1982

Langston Hughes (1902–1967) is one of the best-known African-American writers of our century. He wrote stories, poems, plays, song lyrics, and nonfiction.

What do you picture when you think about autumn? Falling leaves? Chilly weather? Shorter days and longer nights? This story is about Bill and Mary, two people who were once in love. As you read, think about the title of the story. Why does the story take place in the fall?

Early Autumn

Langston Hughes

When Bill was very young, they had been in love. Many nights they had spent walking, talking together. Then something not very important had come between them, and they didn't speak. Impulsively,[1] she had married a man she thought she loved. Bill went away, bitter about women.

Yesterday, walking across Washington Square,[2] she saw him for the first time in years.

"Bill Walker," she said.

He stopped. At first he did not recognize her, to him she looked so old.

"Mary! Where did you come from?"

---

[1] suddenly and without much thought
[2] a park in New York City

Unconsciously,[3] she lifted her face as though wanting a kiss, but he held out his hand. She took it.

"I live in New York now," she said.

"Oh"—smiling politely. Then a little frown came quickly between his eyes.

"Always wondered what happened to you, Bill."

"I'm a lawyer. Nice firm, way downtown."

"Married yet?"

"Sure. Two kids."

"Oh," she said.

A great many people went past them through the park. People they didn't know. It was late afternoon. Nearly sunset. Cold.

"And your husband?" he asked her.

"We have three children. I work in the bursar's[4] office at Columbia."[5]

"You're looking very . . ." (he wanted to say *old*) ". . . well," he said.

She understood. Under the trees in Washington Square, she found herself desperately reaching back into the past. She had been older than he then in Ohio. Now she was not young at all. Bill was still young.

"We live on Central Park West," she said. "Come and see us sometime."

"Sure," he replied. "You and your husband must have dinner with my family some night. Any night. Lucille and I'd love to have you."

The leaves fell slowly from the trees in the Square. Fell without wind. Autumn dusk. She felt a little sick.

"We'd love it," she answered.

"You ought to see my kids." He grinned.

---

[3]without thinking
[4]treasurer's
[5]Columbia University

Suddenly the lights came on up the whole length of Fifth Avenue, chains of misty brilliance in the blue air.

"There's my bus," she said.

He held out his hand, "Good-by."

"When . . ." she wanted to say, but the bus was ready to pull off. The lights on the avenue blurred, twinkled, blurred. And she was afraid to open her mouth as she entered the bus. Afraid it would be impossible to utter a word.

Suddenly she shrieked very loudly, "Good-by!" But the bus door had closed.

The bus started. People came between them outside, people crossing the street, people they didn't know. Space and people. She lost sight of Bill. Then she remembered she had forgotten to give him her address—or to ask him for his—or tell him that her youngest boy was named Bill, too.

REFLECT ·

Why is it surprising that both Bill and Mary are living in New York City?

Is Bill still in love with Mary? How do you know?

The last sentence of the story says that Mary named her youngest son after Bill. What does this tell you about her feelings for Bill Walker? Is Mary still attracted to him? How can you tell?

The writer of "Early Autumn" could have had the story take place at any time of year and day in any kind of weather. But he chose to have Bill and Mary meet on a cold fall day as the sun is setting. Why?

Much of the story is dialogue—two people talking to each other. Try reading the story out loud, as if you were reading a play or a movie script. If you could make a movie of "Early Autumn," which actors would you choose to play Bill and Mary?

WRITE ·······································

What do you think Mary would write in her diary after her surprise meeting with Bill? Imagine that you are Mary, and write a few sentences about what it was like to see Bill again. If you want, use the following beginning to start the diary entry.

October 1
Today I ran into Bill in Washington Square. It was quite a surprise to see him again after all these years. I felt so . . .

It seems to bother Mary that Bill thinks she looks old. Write about a time when you changed the way you looked because of something someone said or did. What did you change? Your weight? Hairstyle? Style of clothes? Something else? Did you feel better after the change? Why or why not?

Think of someone from your past that you would like to see again. What would he or she look like? What would the two of you do and say if you ran into each other? Write a short story about a surprise meeting between the two of you.

Alfred, Lord Tennyson once wrote, "Tis better to have loved and lost / Than never to have loved at all." Do you agree with this statement? Even if a breakup is painful, is it better to have loved someone for a while than never to have loved the person? Explain what you think, giving examples to show what you mean.

How would you feel if you ran across an ex-girlfriend's or ex-boyfriend's wedding announcement while thumbing through a newspaper? As you read, think about how the speaker—the person in the poem—feels.

The Sunday News

Dana Gioia

Looking for something in the Sunday paper,
I flipped by accident through *Local Weddings*,
Yet missed the photograph until I saw
Your name among the headings.

And there you were, looking almost unchanged,
Your hair still long, though now long out of style,
And you still wore that stiff and serious look
You called a smile.

I felt as though we sat there face to face.
My stomach tightened. I read the item through.
It said too much about both families,
Too little about you.

Finished at last, I threw the paper down,
Stung by jealousy, my mind aflame,
Hating this man, this stranger whom you loved,
This printed name.

And yet I clipped it out to put away
Inside a book like something I might use,
A scrap I knew I wouldn't read again
Yet couldn't bear to lose.

REFLECT ·

What first caught the speaker's eye while looking at the wedding announcements in the newspaper?

Was the speaker surprised to read that the ex-girlfriend had gotten married? How do you know?

Does the speaker still care about the ex-girlfriend? How do you know?

Explain why the speaker decided to save the wedding announcement.

WRITE ·

What would happen if the speaker of "The Sunday News" called the ex-girlfriend? What do you think they would say to each other? Write a conversation for the two.

Many people like to keep mementos of important events in their lives. For example, a business owner might frame the first dollar his or her company earns. Or parents might bronze their child's first pair of shoes. Describe a memento that you have kept for a long time, and tell why it is important to you.

Why do people put announcements of their wedding in the newspaper? Explain why you would—or would not—choose to have your wedding reported in your local paper.

Morris Kantor, *Baseball at Night*, 1934
National Museum of American Art, Washington, D.C.
Photograph: Art Resource, New York

*Have you ever wished for a lucky break
that would change your life? This story is
about Pete Maneri, a minor-league baseball player who is waiting for his lucky
break—a chance to play in the majors.
W. C. Heinz, the writer of this story, used
to cover sports for the New York* Sun. *In
"One Throw," he shows us the world of
scouts—people who look for talented ath-
letes to play in the major leagues. As you
read the story, think about the title. What
is the "one throw" the title refers to?*

One Throw

W. C. Heinz

I checked into a hotel called the Olympia, which is
right on the main street and the only hotel in the town.
After lunch I was hanging around the lobby, and I got
to talking to the guy at the desk. I asked him if this
wasn't the town where that kid named Maneri played
ball.

"That's right," the guy said. "He's a pretty good
ballplayer."

"He should be," I said. "I read that he was the new
Phil Rizzuto."[1]

"That's what they said," the guy said.

"What's the matter with him?" I said. "I mean if
he's such a good ballplayer what's he doing in this
league?"

---

[1] a star shortstop for the New York Yankees during the 1940s
and 1950s

"I don't know," the guy said. "I guess the Yankees know what they're doing."

"What kind of a kid is he?"

"He's a nice kid," the guy said. "He plays good ball, but I feel sorry for him. He thought he'd be playing for the Yankees soon, and here he is in this town. You can see it's got him down."

"He lives here in this hotel?"

"That's right," the guy said. "Most of the older ballplayers stay in rooming houses,[2] but Pete and a couple other kids live here."

He was leaning on the desk, talking to me and looking across the hotel lobby. He nodded his head. "This is a funny thing," he said. "Here he comes now."

The kid had come through the door from the street. He had on a light gray sport shirt and a pair of gray flannel slacks.

I could see why, when he showed up with the Yankees in spring training, he made them all think of Rizzuto. He isn't any bigger than Rizzuto, and he looks just like him.

"Hello, Nick," he said to the guy at the desk.

"Hello, Pete," the guy at the desk said. "How goes it today?"

"All right," the kid said but you could see he was exaggerating.

"I'm sorry, Pete," the guy at the desk said, "but no mail today."

"That's all right, Nick," the kid said. "I'm used to it."

"Excuse me," I said, "but you're Pete Maneri?"

"That's right," the kid said, turning and looking at me.

---

[2]houses with rooms that people can rent to live in

"Excuse me," the guy at the desk said, introducing us. "Pete, this is Mr. Franklin."

"Harry Franklin," I said.

"I'm glad to know you," the kid said, shaking my hand.

"I recognize you from your pictures," I said.

"Pete's a good ballplayer," the guy at the desk said.

"Not very," the kid said.

"Don't take his word for it, Mr. Franklin," the guy said.

"I'm a great ball fan," I said to the kid. "Do you people play tonight?"

"We play two games," the kid said.

"The first game's at six o'clock," the guy at the desk said. "They play pretty good ball."

"I'll be there," I said. "I used to play a little ball myself."

"You did?" the kid said.

"With Columbus," I said. "That's twenty years ago."

"Is that right?" the kid said. . . .

That's the way I got to talking with the kid. They had one of those pine-paneled taprooms[3] in the basement of the hotel, and we went down there. I had a couple and the kid had a Coke, and I told him a few stories and he turned out to be a real good listener.

"But what do you do now, Mr. Franklin?" he said after a while.

"I sell hardware," I said. "I can think of some things I'd like better, but I was going to ask you how you like playing in this league."

---

[3]bars

"Well," the kid said, "I suppose it's all right. I guess I've got no kick[4] coming."

"Oh, I don't know," I said. "I understand you're too good for this league. What are they trying to do to you?"

"I don't know," the kid said. "I can't understand it."

"What's the trouble?"

"Well," the kid said, "I don't get along very well here. I mean there's nothing wrong with my playing. I'm hitting .365 right now. I lead the league in stolen bases. There's nobody can field with me, but who cares?"

"Who manages this ball club?"

"Al Dall," the kid said. "You remember, he played in the outfield for the Yankees for about four years."

"I remember."

"Maybe he is all right," the kid said, "but I don't get along with him. He's on my neck all the time."

"Well," I said, "that's the way they are in the minors sometimes. You have to remember the guy is looking out for himself and his ball club first. He's not worried about you."

"I know that," the kid said. "If I get the big hit or make the play he never says anything. The other night I tried to take second on a loose ball and I got caught in the run-down. He bawls me out in front of everybody. There's nothing I can do."

"Oh, I don't know," I said. "This is probably a guy who knows he's got a good thing in you, and he's looking to keep you around. You people lead the league, and that makes him look good. He doesn't want to lose you to Kansas City or the Yankees."

---

[4]complaint

"That's what I mean," the kid said. "When the Yankees sent me down here they said, 'Don't worry. We'll keep an eye on you.' So Dall never sends a good report on me. Nobody ever comes down to look me over. What chance is there for a guy like Eddie Brown or somebody like that coming down to see me in this town?"

"You have to remember that Eddie Brown's the big shot," I said, "the great Yankee scout."

"Sure," the kid said. "I never even saw him, and I'll never see him in this place. I have an idea that if they ever ask Dall about me he keeps knocking me down."

"Why don't you go after Dall?" I said. "I had trouble like that once myself, but I figured out a way to get attention."

"You did?" the kid said.

"I threw a couple of balls over the first baseman's head," I said. "I threw a couple of games away, and that really got the manager sore. I was lousing up his ball club and his record. So what does he do? He blows the whistle on me, and what happens? That gets the brass[5] curious, and they send down to see what's wrong."

"Is that so?" the kid said. "What happened?"

"Two weeks later," I said, "I was up with Columbus."

"Is that right?" the kid said.

"Sure," I said, egging him on. "What have you got to lose?"

"Nothing," the kid said. "I haven't got anything to lose."

"I'd try it," I said.

---

[5]top management

"I might try it," the kid said. "I might try it tonight if the spot comes up."

I could see from the way he said it that he was madder than he'd said. Maybe you think this is mean to steam a kid up like this, but I do some strange things.

"Take over," I said. "Don't let this guy ruin your career."

"I'll try it," the kid said. "Are you coming out to the park tonight?"

"I wouldn't miss it," I said. "This will be better than making out route sheets and sales orders."

It's not much ball park in this town—old wooden bleachers and an old wooden fence and about four hundred people in the stands. The first game wasn't much either, with the home club winning something like 8 to 1.

The kid didn't have any hard chances, but I could see he was a ballplayer, with a double and a couple of walks and a lot of speed.

The second game was different, though. The other club got a couple of runs and then the home club picked up three runs in one, and they were in the top of the ninth with a 3–2 lead and two outs when the pitching began to fall apart and they loaded the bases.

I was trying to wish the ball down to the kid, just to see what he'd do with it, when the batter drives one on one big bounce to the kid's right.

The kid was off for it when the ball started. He made a backhand stab and grabbed it. He was deep now, and he turned in the air and fired. If it goes over the first baseman's head, it's two runs in and a panic—but it's the prettiest throw you'd want to see. It's right on a line, and the runner is out by a step, and it's the ball game.

I walked back to the hotel, thinking about the kid. I sat around the lobby until I saw him come in, and then I walked toward the elevator like I was going to my room, but so I'd meet him. And I could see he didn't want to talk.

"How about a Coke?" I said.

"No," he said. "Thanks, but I'm going to bed."

"Look," I said. "Forget it. You did the right thing. Have a Coke."

We were sitting in the taproom again. The kid wasn't saying anything.

"Why didn't you throw that ball away?" I said.

"I don't know," the kid said. "I had it in my mind before he hit it, but I couldn't."

"Why?"

"I don't know why."

"I know why," I said.

The kid didn't say anything. He just sat looking down.

"Do you know why you couldn't throw that ball away?" I said.

"No," the kid said.

"You couldn't throw that ball away," I said, "because you're going to be a major-league ballplayer someday."

The kid just looked at me. He had that same sore expression.

"Do you know why you're going to be a major-league ballplayer?" I said.

The kid was just looking down again, shaking his head. I never got more of a kick out of anything in my life.

"You're going to be a major-league ballplayer," I said, "because you couldn't throw that ball away, and because I'm not a hardware salesman and my name's not Harry Franklin."

"What do you mean?" the kid said.

"I mean," I explained to him, "that I tried to needle you into throwing that ball away because I'm Eddie Brown."

REFLECT ·

Pete seems eager to know if he received any mail. What letter is he hoping to receive?

Who does Eddie Brown pretend to be?

Why does Eddie pretend to be someone else?

Eddie tells Pete about a way to get management's attention. What does Eddie tell Pete to do?

Eddie's advice to Pete can be seen as a kind of test. What is Eddie testing?

Does Pete pass Eddie's test? Why or why not?

Were you surprised by the ending of the story? Why or why not?

WRITE ·

Pete Maneri is compared to the famous shortshop Phil Rizzuto. Who is a sports hero today? Write a short letter to your favorite sports star, explaining why you look up to him or her.

Pete hopes to get a lucky break. What lucky break would you like to get? A million dollars? Your own business? Fame? Describe the lucky break you would like to get and how you would feel if you got it.

To see what kind of a person Pete is, Eddie tries to get Pete to throw a game (lose a game on purpose). Is Eddie wrong to tempt Pete in this way? Or is it OK since, in the end, Eddie helps Pete? Explain why you think Eddie is right—or wrong.

Have you ever held back from telling somebody the truth to keep from upsetting the person? As you read this poem, think about the young soldier and his feelings toward his parents.

The soldier is fighting in Vietnam, a country in Southeast Asia. The United States was involved in a very unpopular war in Vietnam from the 1950s to the middle 1970s. Larry Rottmann, the writer of the poem, is a Vietnam vet.

APO[1] *96225*

Larry Rottmann

A young man once went off to war
in a far country.
When he had time, he wrote home and
said, "Sure rains here a lot."

But his mother, reading between the lines,[2]
Wrote, "We're quite concerned. Tell us
what it's really like."

And the young man responded, "Wow, you ought
to see the funny monkeys!"

To which the mother replied, "Don't
hold back, how is it?"

---

[1]APO is short for Army Post Office; the title refers to a
soldier's address
[2]thinking about what her son might be holding back

And the young man wrote, "The sunsets here
are spectacular."

In her next letter the mother
wrote, "Son we want you to tell us
everything."

So the next time he wrote,
"Today I killed a man.
Yesterday I helped drop napalm[3] on women and
children. Tomorrow we are going to use
gas."

And the father wrote, "Please don't
write such depressing letters. You're upsetting
your mother."

So, after a while, the young man wrote, "Sure rains a
lot here . . ."

---

[3]mixture used in firebombs

REFLECT ·······································

What three facts about Vietnam does the soldier tell in his first letters home?

Why does he hold back telling his parents about what is happening in the war?

Why does the soldier's mother insist that the soldier write about the war?

Do his parents really want to know the truth about what is happening in the war? Why or why not?

We are given the soldier's address but not his name. Why might the poet have decided to leave the soldier and his family nameless?

WRITE ·······································

Soldiers enjoy getting letters. Explain why letters from home are so important to them.

Write about a time when you held back from telling somebody the truth to keep from upsetting the person. Do you think you made the right decision? Why or why not?

Like the soldier in the poem, do you sometimes hold back from telling family or friends the truth? Or are you a completely honest person in your relationships with family and friends? Explain which kind of person you are.

The poem ends with the soldier writing a letter that says, "Sure rains a lot here . . ." What do you think the soldier's parents write in their letter back to him? Write a few more lines for the poem, telling what you think the parents say in answer to their son's letter.

Red Grooms, *Hooks*, 1980
Copyright 1991 Red Grooms/ARS, New York
Photograph courtesy of Marlborough Gallery, New York City

How do you cope when everything seems wrong? Toby Heckler has a very unusual way of dealing with his problems. As you read the story, you may feel as if you are breaking a code. You might have to read out loud to figure out what Toby is spelling. Once you know what words Toby writes, ask yourself, What makes Toby write tickets?

Tickits

Paul Milenski

Toby Heckler placed the slip of yellow paper under the windshield wiper of the black Oldsmobile that straddled two parking spaces. On the yellow paper Toby had printed in red ink "PRAKING MISTEAK" and signed his name "TOBY" in a childish-looking hand. He snapped the cover on his Pilot Razor Point, slipped the pen over his ear, put the pad of yellow papers in his jacket pocket. He moved down Main Street, his chin held high, his sneakers spanking white from Baby's Liquid Shoe Polish.

As Toby passed Thom McAn,[1] he looked in the window, caught the reflection of his sneakers, looked down at them, moved his toes inside. He straightened the pen on his ear, patted the pad of yellow papers in his pocket, moved along. People stared at Toby; he kept his chin high.

Near the First National Bank two elderly ladies waited for the bus. They stood in the middle of the

---

[1] a shoe store

sidewalk away from the curb. Toby pulled out his pad, slipped the pen off his ear, held the cap with his teeth. He printed slowly, meticulously,[2] then handed one of the ladies the slip, "TO MUSH IN WAY" signed "TOBY." He secured his instruments, walked along as before. The two ladies examined the slip of paper, moved closer to the curb.

At the intersection of Main and South the pedestrian crossing light shone bright orange, "DON'T WALK." Traffic moved, people stood on the curb. A man with a pin-striped suit and briefcase stepped off the curb, was about to sneak across between cars. Toby began to reach for his pad. The cars closed together; the man stepped back to the curb. Toby brought his hand back. When the green light read "WALK," Toby and the man crossed. The man went into a shop. Toby waited for him, handed him a slip as he came out, "ALLMOST WALKD."

Patrolman McVee stood in front of Charlie's Tobacco Shop; McVee's badge number was 635. Toby stopped, stood next to him. McVee looked over.

"How's it going, Toby?" McVee said.

Toby pulled out his pad, showed it to McVee.

"Lots of business, eh Toby?"

Toby put his pad back, nodded. His eyes rolled, looked tortured.

"Yes, Toby, it's a bitch," McVee said.

Toby looked at McVee's shoes. Except for a single smudge they were shiny, black. Toby bent down, rubbed off the smudge with his hand.

"Thanks Toby," McVee said.

Toby caught McVee's eye, looked down at his own sneakers.

---

[2]very carefully

"Very nice, Toby. Spiffy," McVee said.

Toby raised his chin again, moved along.

Before the rain came, Toby had used up half his pad. Near Mario's Grinders there was a dog tied to a parking meter; he had wrapped his leash tightly around the pole. Toby stuck a slip under his collar, "TYED WORNG." Toby walked into the YMCA, handed the man at the desk a slip, "Y BORKEN." On a Park Square bench a man ate a candy bar; he threw his wrapper down. Toby handed him the wrapper and a slip, "PAPUR ON GARSS." The man walked away throwing both papers down. Toby caught up to him, gave him all the papers and another slip, "NOT LISSEN-ING." The man said "Christ," put all the papers in his pocket.

The rain began to wet Toby's slips, blot his ink. He put everything away, looked up at the sky, rolled his eyes.

By the time he got back to Main and South, it was raining hard. A car moved through the intersection, splashed dirty water on his sneakers. Toby walked quickly down South, cut through the alley between Sam's Auto Supplies and Blue Arc Welding, avoided puddles on Mill, moved along the flood control wall on River, came to his bungalow,[3] entered.

Inside there were smells of cabbage, cigarette smoke, spilt alcohol. The entry was dark, lit intermittently[4] with a pale light from the television. He knew his mother lay on the sofa, smoking, drinking, surrounded by TV magazines. The sofa with a large hump cast a shadow on the wall.

---

[3]one-story house
[4]on and off

Toby took off his sneakers, carried them up the stairs.

His mother turned her head, "Toby, is that you?" Her voice was raspy, tired. But Toby was already in his room, the door closed, Baby's Liquid Shoe Polish in front of him on the floor.

His mother moved to the bottom of the stairs. She coughed, yelled, "Toby!"

Toby opened the door, showed himself to his mother.

She held a cigarette and a drink. "Toby, you could've been a goddamn burglar sneaking around me like that!" Toby closed the door, reached under his bed.

"Toby, you goddamn nut!"

Toby pulled out a shoebox. On the cover it read, "MUTHERS TICKITS."

Toby wrote three slips: "TO MUSH SOMKING," "TO MUSH DIRNKING," "TOO MUSH YELING." He placed the slips in the box. Then, before he put the box away, he wrote one more slip in his largest letters: "ERVYTHING WORNG!"

With the box safely under his bed, Toby sat on the floor, bit his tongue, went to polishing his sneakers spanking white.

REFLECT ·

Toby writes and hands out several tickets. What does each ticket say?

Toby gives tickets to people when they make small mistakes. What are some other times in the story when Toby is picky about details?

Put yourself in Toby's place. What problems might you have if you could not speak? How might you feel about yourself? About other people?

Toby writes tickets to his mother, but he does not give them to her. What does this tell you about their relationship?

Why does Toby write tickets?

WRITE ·

Who would you like to give a ticket to? Pick two people, and write a ticket to each person.

Explain what you do to cope when everything seems to be going wrong.

Which are you: someone who likes to be in control or someone who likes others to do the controlling? Think of your relationships at home, work, or school. Then explain which type of person you are.

Have you ever needed to phone someone for help in an emergency? As you read the poem, picture the two people talking on the phone. How do they feel about each other?

Collect Calls

Diana Bickston

I called my mother in 1979
I told her I was in jail
Would she send money?
"The roof is leaking, the house is a wreck,
took out a second mortgage, we're
up to our ears in debt. I'll write
when I can and on that
you can bet. Call anytime
Just don't call collect."

I called my mother in 1980,
I told her I had escaped,
Would she send money?
"I work only part time, the bills
are in stacks. The car needs repairing;
we can't pay the tax. I can loan you $20."

I called my mother in 1981.
I told her I was dying
from the bullet of a police gun.
The phone hung in silence and
then she began
      "Where is my twenty
      and why did you run?"

REFLECT ·

What happened to the caller in 1979? 1980? 1981?

Why does the mother say not to call collect?

Do you think it would have made a difference in the caller's life if the mother had helped out? Why or why not?

Read the poem out loud and with feeling. Notice that the mother's words rhyme. What do the rhymes tell you about the mother's attitude toward the caller?

WRITE ·

Has there ever been a time when you really needed help, and it wasn't there? What did you do? Describe the problem and how you solved it.

The mother gives several reasons that she cannot lend money to the caller. What would you say if your best friend asked you for rent money? Explain why you would say yes—or no.

We are never told why the caller is in prison. Imagine what might have happened, and explain what the caller did to end up in jail.

Peter Stäempfli, *Riviera, No. 4,* 1968
Galerie Lelong, Zurich

Do you know people who cause problems for themselves because of the way they treat others? Maybe you've heard the saying, "That person's just asking for trouble." Something happens to Harry Joe Shreve's car at the Speed Cleen Car Wash. As you read, ask yourself why Shreve's car was "chosen."

Speed Cleen

James Stevenson

"Don't forget those little ashtrays in the back, my friend!" called Harry Joe Shreve, holding open the front door of his white Chrysler Imperial. The windows of the car were shut, so he couldn't call through the window ("TURN OFF ENGINE. LEAVE CAR IN NEUTRAL. CLOSE WINDOWS," said the sign above the door of the Speed Cleen Car Wash), but the car-wash attendant who was crouched down vacuuming the floor behind the front seat gave no sign of hearing. "Ashtrays, boy!" called Shreve, louder, and when the man turned his dark, blank face toward him Shreve pointed at the ashtrays. Then he closed the door and stepped back. A second attendant—a tall, skinny man wearing Army-surplus clothes, a cap, and black rubber boots—was shooting steam from a hose at the wheels of the Chrysler, and Shreve, walking around the front of his car, tried to call his attention to the left headlight, which had a small mark on it—a black, V-shaped smear that looked like oil—but the man, when he looked over, merely nodded. "Well, come on take a *look*!" called Shreve. "I'm showing you what I'm talking about." The man continued to shoot steam at the wheels, so Shreve, his face reddening, strode over and grabbed him by the arm. "Come here," he said, and led him around the front of the car. "See what I'm talking about?" he said, pointing to the mark on the rim of the light. "You see?" The man gazed evenly at it, the steam hose spitting at the ground beside him. Shreve made a rubbing motion with his free hand. "You clean that good, hear?" Then he let go of the man's arm and stepped back, shaking his head. "What's the use?" he said to himself. Another attendant, this one in a faded sweatshirt, was attaching a small chain to the front bumper of the Chrysler; the chain was attached in turn to a thicker, heavier chain that crawled forward— gleaming with grease—along the floor of the car wash. Presently, the white Chrysler began to inch slowly into the building, following a bright-red Buick Riviera. The Buick disappeared into the steam clouds, and Shreve's car moved after it. Shreve had a last glimpse of his Alabama plate,[1] and then a black Cadillac Eldorado was hauled by, blocking his view. Shreve watched for a moment, staring at the churning clouds, the shower of hot water, and—when the steam parted for an instant—the giant spinning brushes.

Shreve turned away and walked along the side of the building toward the front of the car wash. Beyond a chain fence was the deserted parking lot of a frozen-custard[2] stand. "SEE YOU IN THE SPRING," said a sign on one of the big windows, but the place had a desolate, bankrupt[3] look. Across the highway was a discount furniture store. At the end of the fence, by the front of the car wash, there were several black oil

---

[1]Alabama license plate
[2]ice cream
[3]out of business

drums with wringers, and men with rolled-up sleeves, breathing steam, were plunging rags into the drums, wringing them out, and then scrubbing and polishing the chrome on the newly washed cars that emerged[4] from the building. The car owners stood around, watching, waiting.

Shreve glanced into the car wash. The red Buick was just visible, covered with soapsuds, behind several other cars, but the Chrysler was still out of sight. The nearest car—a green Ford—was moving under the hot-air dryer, flecks of water leaping from its roof and hood. Shreve walked along the sidewalk, lighting a cigarette. Next to the car wash was an auto-parts store, its windows smeared with dirt; there were stacks of tires and bumpers and accessories piled in the dimness. Two hundred yards down the highway were the big blue turnpike[5] signs. Shreve glanced at his watch. A few minutes more—five, maybe—and he'd be back on the turnpike, homeward bound. He turned back to the car wash just in time to see the red Buick emerging, gleaming in the sunlight. He strode over and peered into the building to see how his Chrysler looked. There, a few feet behind the rear of the red Buick, coming slowly along on the chain, was the black Cadillac. Behind it was a blue Volkswagen, and behind that a gray Rover. "Where's my car?" said Shreve, almost to himself. Then he yelled, "Where's my car!" He ran into the building. The floor was slippery with oil and water, and it was hot inside. "My car!" he yelled. "Where is it?" The faces of the attendants were blank, puzzled. He ran all the way through the building, past the unfamiliar cars, past the hot-air dryer and the hot-

---

[4]came out
[5]expressway

water rinse and the soapy brushes and the steam, and then he was outdoors again, where he had started a few minutes before. "Where is my car?" he demanded of the tall, thin man in the Army-surplus clothes. "What's the big idea?"

"What car?" said the man.

"My Imperial!" yelled Shreve. "My Chrysler Imperial!"

The man looked puzzled, and shook his head slowly. "I didn't see no Chrysler Imperial," he said.

"You cleaned it!" yelled Shreve. "I saw you clean it! I saw you clean my car!"

The man shook his head. "I don't recall no Imperial," he said.

Shreve spun around and pointed at the man with the vacuum. "You cleaned it, too," he said. "I told you 'Clean the ashtrays'! Remember—the ashtrays!"

The attendant frowned. "Don't remember no Imperial today," he said.

"But it went on the chain!" Shreve shouted. "I saw it hooked on right in front of that black Caddy. One of you must have taken it off while it was inside there."

"You can't take no car off that chain, Mister," the attendant said. "That chain's movin' all the time. It's hot in there. All that steam and stuff—you can see." He shook his head and turned slowly away, opening the door of the next car in line.

"Where's the manager?" demanded Shreve, running back inside the building. No one paid any attention. When he emerged on the front sidewalk, his clothes damp from the sprays, the men were putting the final touches on the black Cadillac. Shreve grabbed a short, stout man who was polishing the rear bumper. "Where's the manager?"

"He went away for a while."

"My car's gone," said Shreve.

"You got your ticket?" asked the short man.

"What ticket?" yelled Shreve. "I didn't get any ticket!"

"Got to have the ticket," said the man. "Didn't nobody give you the ticket when you come in?"

"No!" Shreve was beginning to feel dizzy.

The short man glanced around and caught the eye of the Cadillac owner—a man in a dark suit and hat, wearing glasses. "You got *your* ticket, Mister?" he asked.

The man pulled his hand from his coat pocket and held up a small, pink ticket.

Shreve stepped over to him. "They didn't *give* me a ticket," he said.

The man turned away, shrugging slightly.

"They took my car," said Shreve.

"I don't know anything about that," said the man.

"All set, sir," said the short attendant, and the man handed him the ticket and two dollars, and got into the Cadillac, slamming the door. Shreve ran over to the car.

"Listen, friend," he said, "I'm from out of state. They—"

The window of the Cadillac rolled quietly and quickly closed, and then the car was moving away, out onto the highway. Shreve watched it drive away down the road, and then he turned back. The attendants were all busy now on the Volkswagen. No one looked at him. Shreve yelled, "I'm going to get the police, you hear? The police!"

He turned and started to stride down the sidewalk, not caring which way he was going, just getting out of there, going to find a phone. He was in front of the auto-parts store now—they might have a phone he could use—and he grabbed the door handle. It was locked. "CLOSED FOR VACATION," said a hand-lettered

sign on the door. Shreve peered through the dirty
window of the dark store, swearing, and he was about
to turn away when he saw, on top of a heap of bumpers
and tires, a single headlight—one with a small, V-
shaped black smear on the rim that looked like oil.

REFLECT ·

Imagine that you have been asked to help solve the
"case of the missing car." Using clues from the story,
explain what happened to Shreve's automobile.

Why didn't Shreve get a ticket? Who decided not to
give him one?

Why might the car-wash attendants prefer to steal the
car of an out-of-towner?

Do you feel sorry for Shreve? Why or why not?

Why is Speed Cleen a fitting name for the car wash?

WRITE ································

Have you ever lost something valuable? Describe what you lost, and explain how you felt.

Imagine that you are a new worker at the Speed Cleen Car Wash. What do you see happening to some people's cars? How? Why? Write a letter to a friend telling what really happens at work. If you want, use the following beginning to get started.

> Dear Friend,
>
> You wouldn't believe what's been going on at the car wash where I work. The boss makes money not only by running a car wash, but also by running a . . .

Read a few police reports from a newspaper in your area. Then write a short police report about what happened at the Speed Cleen Car Wash.

Can you really make a difference in the world? Rosa Parks proved that you can.

In 1955, she was arrested in Montgomery, Alabama, for breaking a city law that said blacks had to sit in the back of public buses. After her arrest, blacks boycotted the Montgomery bus system for a year.

As you read, think about the people who took part in the boycott. For months, they walked rather than ride the buses. What made them do it?

Montgomery

for rosa parks

Sam Cornish

white woman have you heard
she is too tired to sit in the back
her feet two hundred years old

move to the back or walk
around to the side door how
long can a woman be a cow

your feet will not move
and you never listen
but even if it rains empty
seats will ride through town

i walk for my children
my feet two hundred years old

REFLECT ·

Is the speaker a black person or a white person? How do you know?

The speaker says, "she is too tired to sit in the back / her feet two hundred years old." Who is the speaker talking about? Why does the speaker say the person's feet are two hundred years old?

Why will "empty seats" ride through town?

Why does the speaker say, "I walk for my children"?

WRITE ·

Imagine that you are a reporter writing a story about Rosa Parks. Write a list of at least three questions that you would like to ask her in an interview.

Rosa Parks helped change the world. If you could change the world, what would you change? Describe a problem you would like to see solved.

"It is OK to break a law if the law is unfair." Do you agree or disagree with this statement? Explain what you think.

Roland Petersen, *San Francisco Interior with Landscape*, 1987
Private Collection
Photograph courtesy of Harcourts Contemporary Gallery,
San Francisco

Have you ever formed an opinion about somebody before you really knew the person? Most people make this mistake from time to time. In this story, two women with very different backgrounds make snap judgments about each other. How do their attitudes change as they get to know each other?

She Said a Bad Word

Jose Yglesias

Mama's paper bag became unstuck at the bottom and a potato got away—at the very moment when she realized that the black girl at the bus stop was one of them.[1] Aha. She had passed her earlier on the way to Angie's store, and thought what funny skirts girls are wearing. And that's all. She'd heard plenty about them being only a block away on Nebraska Avenue but had never seen one.

What was she going to do about the potato? Another one slid out, and two tomatoes and one pepper were in danger.

Mama brought her other arm around the bag and held on, the way she had hugged her belly during her first pregnancy. What must she look like? Her own mother used to laugh at her then. Out of the corner of her eye she saw that shiny little black skirt shaking up to her and creasing even smaller as the girl bent over and picked up the potatoes.

"It's leather!" Mama exclaimed, and the girl's face

---

[1] prostitutes

appeared at the level of her paper bag and said something like ooo-yaw.

Everything must be showing on the other side when she leaned over like that. A passing car honked. Mama straightened and looked stiff, insulted. Automatically, without thinking.

The girl said something unintelligible[2] and flipped a hand with a disdainful motion of her wrist. Mama nodded her angry agreement, though she suspected the girl had used a bad word, and the car moved on.

The vegetables at the bottom were now secure, but the little package of Kleenex fell out the top. The girl picked that up too and another car honked.

This time they laughed.

The girl said something that sounded less angry and Mama said, "You said?" though she figured it was about the boys laughing in the car. Maybe a bad word again, for the girl shrugged and looked down, somewhat ashamed, Mama guessed, of what she'd called the boys, and then shook her head and laughed again.

Mama gaped at her: her lips were thin and prettily shaped, her nose not what people expect. The girl said something that sounded mild and gave her body a wriggly shake. But Mama still didn't understand, and she was going to ask if she was from up north, New York or Cleveland, where two of her children lived, when the girl laughed once more and held up the potatoes in one hand and the Kleenexes in the other, like a girl in a TV commercial.

Then miraculously the words came through clearly. The girl said, "Ain't no car gonna offer me a ride with me like this." But Mama still gaped and she became unintelligible again.

---

[2]unclear; impossible to understand

She wore a fuzzy pink puffball of a sweater. No sleeves but a sweater nevertheless. It brought Mama out of her trance. After all, it was Florida in May. "Aren't you hot in that?"

She looked Mama in the eye—a little mean that look—and laughed an evil laugh.

Mama couldn't have explained why but she laughed too.

Immediately the girl became understandable. "No way you can carry that mothern bag. Where ya goin'?" Mama indicated her block across the street. "I'll carry the Kleenexes and the potatoes—wheee! Let 'em think I'm a homebody."

For the first time Mama saw that the little leather skirt didn't meet the sweater. No sir. That supple stretch was no belt but her flesh, and right in the middle where the buckle should have been, believe it or not, her navel.

Mama wanted to say no to be polite, the way Latins like her had been taught, but nodded twice because the girl might misunderstand. One, because she was black. Two, because she was—well, maybe she wasn't. But anyway, there was no stopping the girl. She said her name was Lula, led Mama across Nebraska faster than Mama had walked in a long time, then slowed down those long shining black legs (did she oil them?) to stay in step with Mama and asked, "You be one of these Puerto Ricans from down here?" All this just as Mama began to worry what the old women on her block would think seeing them go by together.

Mama said, "No." It came out in a little gasp because one, she wasn't Puerto Rican, and two, she saw Melba raise her fat behind from her glider,[3] her staring

---

[3]porch swing

eyes round as marbles. "My mother was brought here from Spain when she was a baby and my father came from Cuba."

Lula thought it over. "That make you Hispanic. You know, like TV when they tell you how many outta work. This many black, this many Hispanic?"

Mama still felt like objecting but she had to nod. You could call her Hispanic, wasn't that funny.

Lula caught her hesitation and again said something unintelligible.

"You said?" Mama said, putting on a smile for the sake of Chela directly across the street from staring Melba—she was falling into her rose bushes, in a manner of speaking. She would be the first to tell her daughter Vilma.

It gave her a queasy feeling to think of Vilma now—fifty and still a good unmarried girl off on her third vacation away from her, traveling with other decent single girls like her, this time to Hawaii. Even when Vilma was a teenager and they used to take her to Clearwater Beach, she hadn't displayed as much flesh swimming as Lula did waiting for a bus.

"Bettern a cracker," Lula said.

Mama laughed out loud at that and heard a screen door open on their side of the block. It was Alice, who never missed a thing, and she came down her porch steps and said, "Everything all right?"

Mama said, "Couldn't be better," and walked on.

Alice's sister Graciela watched from inside, cautious since the black boy came up to her porch asking for directions and reached out and yanked the gold chain from her neck. No more than she deserved for trying to find out whom he was visiting. The most exciting event of the year.

Her own daughter Vilma had said, What can you expect—with all those girls on Nebraska! Vilma didn't like those girls. Mama had named her after Vilma Banky, into whose tent Valentino[4] had crept.

Could this Lula be one of those girls really? Mama looked at her oiled legs and that little skirt. Oh, there was no doubt, and she laughed again.

For the rest of the block Lula didn't become unintelligible again. She told Mama about herself and began by saying she came from Boston. She waved a hand and almost lost a potato. "Tha's a lie. I'm ashamed a Harlem."[5]

"Such a famous place," Mama said.

"You heard somethin' good about it?" Lula said.

They laughed again and Lula said she had come to Florida to visit her grandmother. Her daddy's mother. He had shown up for the first time in years and that's how she found out just where in Florida she had a grandmother. "I gotta tell you I wished it was Miami. But I come to Tampa to try my luck anyway. In Harlem even luck don't have a chance."

"She must be glad to see you," Mama said.

Lula gave a little shriek and followed Mama up the steps to her porch and became unintelligible again. She shook her head toward Nebraska and Mama heard the word *cousin* before her ears stopped functioning again. Mama was afraid Lula didn't like her cousin or her grandmother.

But Lula liked the plants on the porch. She grew some on the fire escape in Harlem. "When I was a kid. No more."

"It's no use here too," Mama said. "They steal them off the porch at night. My daughter Vilma fusses with them. I don't bother."

---

[4]Rudolph Valentino was a famous movie actor in the 1920s. Vilma Banky co-starred with him in *Son of the Shiek*.
[5]section of New York City

"You got a daughter?" Lula said.

So it was Mama's turn and she told her she had children and grandchildren up north and Vilma here living with her. "She never married," Mama said as if Lula had asked.

"I ain't never gonna marry," Lula said. "Never." She placed the potatoes on the porch table where Mama had unloaded her things, then slowly said, "Well," and went back to the steps and looked down the block to Nebraska like a condemned prisoner. "I betta go back there and raise some money to go home."

She didn't look at Mama. It had just come out without her meaning to.

Mama quickly asked her to have some lemonade. "You sit down awhile. I'm all alone. You can catch the next bus."

"Oh yeah, there's always a next bus," Lula said, and gave her that sharp, mean look. "Okay, I sit," and she flopped down on a nylon-webbed aluminum chair.

Last thing Mama saw as she went inside was Lula sitting with her legs stretched out like a boy and the little leather skirt had climbed up her thighs and disappeared. Rosario across the street no doubt could see, as they used to say, all the way to Port Tampa.

She hurried to the kitchen, found the tray Vilma insisted on using even when serving only a glass of water, and poured two glasses from the pitcher in the icebox. She could hear Vilma correct her: Refrigerator, mother.

Poor Vilma.

Vilma liked to bring her lemonade when she sat out on the porch. Vilma liked to fuss. The whole block always knew when Vilma had brought her bad-tempered old mother a glass of lemonade and the old woman hadn't appreciated it.

Poor Vilma.

Vilma never let her walk over to Angie's store, of course, and she would have taken all the groceries directly inside—Mama stopped, transfixed[6] by a new thought, and forgot to close the refrigerator door. She had left her pocketbook out there too. All the spending money Vilma had given her in new bills for the whole two weeks she was going to be away. She was being punished for her bad thoughts about Vilma. She must not run to the porch. That girl wouldn't take it.

Why shouldn't she?

It made her flesh crawl to hold herself back. She picked up the tray but she could not hold it steady. And she hadn't fixed a plate with the Social Tea biscuits. The refrigerator door was open. She put down the tray. She took a deep breath. Was the money in that stupid Christmas wallet lying on top? She told herself to be calm and she did everything she had to do: the crackers on Vilma's pretty Spanish plate, extra ice in a soup bowl.

That black girl was a good girl. She only needed to get back to New York. Mama had some more money, money Vilma didn't know about. It was hidden under the linoleum in her bedroom. That was the way you saved money in the old days when banks folded[7] before an ordinary person could tell. Mama prepared herself for the worst.

She opened the screen door and tried not to look at the pocketbook but she must have because Lula immediately said, "You left your bag. I can see ya

---

[6]lost in thought
[7]went out of business

wallet. I shoulda taken it. Isn't that what we suppose to do?"

Mama didn't know what to say. Lula hadn't said a bad word and she'd heard her clearly: no static. So Mama settled for, "My goodness," and hoped Lula would not become unintelligible.

She did.

Mama pushed the pocketbook off the table and set the tray down in its place.

Lula said, "You mad with it or somethin'?"

Mama leaned over her and said in a low voice, "Lula, do you need some money?"

Static again, then Lula said, "Who doesn't?"

Mama said, "You're funny."

"Tha's how white ladies test cleaning women, leave their money around. Like it's an exam."

Mama wished she could say that she didn't know that. She straightened and looked away and saw that there was some old fool or other out on every porch on the block. All on account of this girl. All looking her way, like bystanders on TV.

"And don't say my goodness," Lula said, "or I'll start in cussin'."

Mama sat down across from Lula's long bare legs and held out the plate with the Social Tea biscuits. "Go ahead. I'm getting so I like cussin'."

Lula gave her her mean look and Mama looked right back without wavering.[8] This was it: take me or leave me. The mean look turned into a smile that showed her perfect, specially white teeth. "You passed my test, you know."

---

[8]changing her expression

Mama said, "Now that's settled—how much money do you need to get back to Harlem?"

Lula took one of the dumb cookies. "You just like my mama. You don't mind your own business." But her beautiful teeth were still in view. "I'm gonna drink your lemonade and tha's enough," she said slowly.

"Well then, tell me all about yourself," Mama said, settling back, sure that Lula would never be unintelligible to her again, ever.

REFLECT ·

How do Mama and Lula meet?

Name times in the story when Lula is guilty of stereotyping—labeling people without knowing them as individuals. Does Mama stereotype people? Do Mama's neighbors? How can you tell?

Mama's feelings about Lula change after the two women get to know each other. What does Mama think of Lula at the end of the story? What does Lula think of Mama?

Why does Lula turn down Mama's offer of money?

WRITE ································

Do people ever make snap judgments about you? Set the record straight by finishing these statements:

- When people first meet me, they think I'm . . .
- But once they know me better, they find out I'm . . .

"You can't judge a book by looking at its cover." Would Mama agree with this old saying? Would Lula? Explain what you think Mama and Lula would say.

What would Mama's daughter Vilma say if she knew that her mother had spent an afternoon with Lula? Write the conversation you think the mother and daughter would have as they argue about Lula.

John Updike has written novels, short stories, poems, and essays. In 1982, he won the Pulitzer Prize for his novel Rabbit Is Rich, *and in 1991, he won his second Pulitzer for* Rabbit at Rest.

Have you ever wondered about the people who lived in your home before you? The speaker of this poem moves into a home and finds items left behind by the people who used to live there. To the speaker, these items are clues to a mystery: what were the previous tenants like? As you read, ask yourself, What makes the speaker write them a note?

Note to the Previous Tenants

John Updike

Thank you for leaving the bar of soap,
the roll of paper towels,
the sponge mop, the bucket.

I tried to scrub the white floor clean,
discovered it impossible,
and realized you had tried too.

Often, no doubt. The long hair in the sink
was a clue to what? Were you
boys or girls or what?

How often did you dance on the floor?
The place was broom clean. Your lives
were a great wind that has swept by.

Thank you; even the dirt
seemed a gift, a continuity[1]
underlying the breaking of leases.

And the soap, green in veins
like meltable marble, and curved
like a bit of an ideal woman.

Lone, I took a bath with your soap
and had no towel not paper ones
and dried in the air like the floor.

---

[1]a link between the past and the present

REFLECT ·

Name the items that the previous tenants left behind.

What do these items tell you about the previous tenants?

The speaker thanks the previous tenants for "continuity." How does the soap create continuity between the speaker and the tenants?

WRITE ·

Imagine that you are packing a "box of memories"— items for your grandchildren to remember you by. Fifty years from today, they will open the box and see what kind of person you were. List five things that you would pack in the box, and write a sentence for each explaining why the item is important to you.

Did people live in your home before you? What would you like to say to them? Write a short letter of thanks—or complaint—to your "previous tenants."

Describe what it is like to walk through an empty new apartment or house for the first time. What do you think you might see as you walk through the place? What sounds might you hear? What odors might you smell?

Henri Matisse, *Tete de Lorette aux deux Meches*, 1917
Private Collection, Copyright 1991 Succesion H. Matisse/ARS,
New York

Have you ever been embarrassed by something that you said or did? People do not want to make fools of themselves in front of others. The man in this story is made to look foolish by strangers. As you read, think about the title of the story. Who is the thief?

Thief

Robley Wilson, Jr.

He is waiting at the airline ticket counter when he first notices the young woman. She has glossy black hair pulled tightly into a knot at the back of her head—the man imagines it loosed and cascading[1] to the small of her back—and carries over the shoulder of her leather coat a heavy black purse. She wears black boots of soft leather. He struggles to see her face—she is ahead of him in line—but it is not until she has bought her ticket and turns to walk away that he realizes her beauty, which is pale and dark-eyed and full-mouthed, and which quickens his heartbeat. She seems aware that he is staring at her and lowers her gaze abruptly.

The airline clerk interrupts. The man gives up looking at the woman—he thinks she may be about twenty-five—and buys a round-trip, coach class ticket to an eastern city.

His flight leaves in an hour. To kill time, the man steps into one of the airport cocktail bars and orders a scotch and water. While he sips it he watches the flow of travelers through the terminal—including a remark-

---

[1]flowing

able number, he thinks, of unattached pretty women dressed in fashion magazine clothes—until he catches sight of the black-haired girl in the leather coat. She is standing near a Travelers Aid counter, deep in conversation with a second girl, a blonde in a cloth coat trimmed with gray fur. He wants somehow to attract the brunette's attention, to invite her to have a drink with him before her own flight leaves for wherever she is traveling, but even though he believes for a moment she is looking his way he cannot catch her eye from out of the shadows of the bar. In another instant the two women separate; neither of their directions is toward him. He orders a second scotch and water.

When next he sees her he is buying a magazine to read during the flight and becomes aware that someone is jostling[2] him. At first he is startled that anyone would be so close as to touch him, but when he sees who it is he musters[3] a smile.

"Busy place," he says.

She looks up at him—Is she blushing?—and an odd grimace[4] crosses her mouth and vanishes. She moves away from him and joins the crowds in the terminal.

The man is at the counter with his magazine, but when he reaches into his back pocket for his wallet the pocket is empty. *Where could I have lost it?* he thinks. His mind begins enumerating[5] the credit cards, the currency, the membership and identification cards; his stomach churns with something very like fear. *The girl who was so near to me,* he thinks—and all at once he understands that she has picked his pocket.

---

[2]lightly pushing
[3]manages to make
[4]disapproving frown
[5]counting

What is he to do? He still has his ticket, safely tucked inside his suitcoat—he reaches into the jacket to feel the envelope, to make sure. He can take the flight, call someone to pick him up at his destination— since he cannot even afford bus fare—conduct his business and fly home. But in the meantime he will have to do something about the lost credit cards—call home, have his wife get the numbers out of the top desk drawer, phone the card companies—so difficult a process, the whole thing suffocating. What shall he do?

First: Find a policeman, tell what has happened, describe the young woman; damn her, he thinks, for seeming to be attentive to him, to let herself stand so close to him, to blush prettily when he spoke—and all the time she wanted only to steal from him. And her blush was not shyness but the anxiety of being caught; that was most disturbing of all. *Damned deceitful[6] creatures.* He will spare the policeman the details— just tell what she has done, what is in the wallet. He grits his teeth. He will probably never see his wallet again.

He is trying to decide if he should save time by talking to a guard near the X-ray machines when he is appalled[7]—and elated[8]—to see the black-haired girl. (*Ebony-Tressed[9] Thief*, the newspapers will say.) She is seated against a front window of the terminal, taxis and private cars moving sluggishly beyond her in the gathering darkness; she seems engrossed in a book. A seat beside her is empty, and the man occupies it.

"I've been looking for you," he says.

---

[6]dishonest
[7]horrified
[8]joyful
[9]black-haired

She glances at him with no sort of recognition. "I don't know you," she says.

"Sure you do."

She sighs and puts the book aside. "Is this all you characters think about?—picking up girls like we were stray animals? What do you think I am?"

"You lifted my wallet," he says. He is pleased to have said "lifted," thinking it sounds more worldly than *stole* or *took* or even *ripped off.*

"I beg your pardon?" the girl says.

"I know you did—at the magazine counter. If you'll just give it back, we can forget the whole thing. If you don't, then I'll hand you over to the police."

She studies him, her face serious. "All right," she says. She pulls the black bag onto her lap, reaches into it and draws out a wallet.

He takes it from her. "Wait a minute," he says. "This isn't mine."

The girl runs; he bolts after her. It is like a scene in a movie—bystanders scattering, the girl zig-zagging to avoid collisions, the sound of his own breathing reminding him how old he is—until he hears a woman's voice behind him:

"Stop, thief! Stop that man!"

Ahead of him the brunette disappears around a corner and in the same moment a young man in a marine uniform puts out a foot to trip him up. He falls hard, banging knee and elbow on the tile floor of the terminal, but manages to hang on to the wallet which is not his.

The wallet is a woman's, fat with money and credit cards from places like Sak's and I. Magnin and Lord & Taylor, and it belongs to the blonde in the fur-trimmed coat—the blonde he has earlier seen in conversation with the criminal brunette. She, too, is breathless, as is the policeman with her.

"That's him," the blonde girl says. "He lifted my billfold."

It occurs to the man that he cannot even prove his own identity to the policeman.

Two weeks later—the embarrassment and rage have diminished,[10] the family lawyer has been paid, the confusion in his household has receded—the wallet turns up without explanation in one morning's mail. It is intact,[11] no money is missing, all the cards are in place. Though he is relieved, the man thinks that for the rest of his life he will feel guilty around policemen, and ashamed in the presence of women.

REFLECT ·

What makes the man first notice the black-haired woman in the airport terminal?

The black-haired woman tricks the man twice. The first time is when she steals his wallet. What is the second time?

What details tell you that the brunette and the blonde are working together?

Why do the women return the man's wallet?

---

[10]lessened
[11]whole; complete

WRITE ····································

The man in the story is embarrassed by the theft. Describe your most embarrassing moment.

Imagine that you are one of the women in the story. Write a letter to the man explaining why you returned his wallet and its contents intact.

"Since the women returned everything they took, no harm was done." Do you agree or disagree with this statement? Explain what you think.

William Stafford has written poems, short stories, and nonfiction. His collection of poems Traveling Through the Dark *won a National Book Award in 1963.*

What comes to mind when you think about being fifteen years old? The teenage years can be a difficult time. Many teenagers feel as if they are caught between two worlds—the world of the child and the world of the adult. As you read, ask yourself, In what ways is the speaker like a child? In what ways like an adult?

Fifteen

William Stafford

South of the bridge on Seventeenth
I found back of the willows one summer
day a motorcycle with engine running
as it lay on its side, ticking over
slowly in the high grass. I was fifteen.

I admired all that pulsing gleam, the
shiny flanks,[1] the demure[2] headlights
fringed where it lay; I led it gently
to the road and stood with that
companion, ready and friendly. I was fifteen.

---

[1]sides
[2]shy

We could find the end of a road, meet
the sky on out Seventeenth. I thought about
hills, and patting the handle got back a
confident opinion. On the bridge we indulged[3]
a forward feeling, a tremble. I was fifteen.

Thinking, back farther in the grass I found
the owner, just coming to, where he had flipped
over the rail. He had blood on his hand, was pale—
I helped him walk to his machine. He ran his hand
over it, called me good man, roared away.

I stood there, fifteen.

REFLECT ·

The speaker finds a motorcycle lying on its side in
the grass. How did it get there? What happened
before the speaker came along?

Does the speaker want to take the motorcycle? How
can you tell?

At what point does the speaker change his mind
about taking the motorcycle? What do his actions tell
you about him?

---

[3]gave in to

The last line is separate from the rest of the poem.
How does this affect the way that you read the line?
How does it affect the meaning of the line?

WRITE ································

What is it like being fifteen years old? Choose one of
the following beginnings, and write about your
teenage years.

- I would like to be fifteen again, because . . .
- I would not like to be fifteen again, because . . .
- The worst thing about being fifteen was . . .
- The best thing about being fifteen was . . .

Like the speaker, most people feel torn between
freedom and responsibility from time to time.
Imagine that you have suddenly been freed of all
responsibilities. Where would you go? What would
you do?

What does it mean to be mature? Write a definition
for the word, and give two or three examples to
explain your definition.

Victory Von Reynonds, *Riding Back from Patrol,* 1969
Courtesy of The United States Army Center of Military History

How does it feel to face up to a fear and overcome it? Perhaps no one knows better than a soldier getting ready to fight. The battle in this story takes place in the Middle East between soldiers from Israel and Syria. Mark Helprin, the writer of the story, has served in the Israeli infantry and air force. Like many authors, he sometimes draws on his experiences when he writes. As you read, put yourself in the soldiers' place. Picture what they see and feel as they wait to fight.

North Light
—A Recollection in the Present Tense

Mark Helprin

We are being held back. We are poised at a curve in the road on the southern ridge of a small valley. The sun shines from behind, illuminating with flawless light the moves and countermoves of several score tanks below us. For a long time, we have been absorbed in the mystery of matching the puffs of white smoke from tank cannon with the sounds that follow. The columns[1] themselves move silently: only the great roar rising from the battle proves it not to be a dream.

A man next to me is deeply absorbed in sniffing his wrist. "What are you doing?" I ask.

"My wife," he says. "I can still smell her perfume on my wrist, and I taste the taste of her mouth. It's sweet."

---

[1] rows of tanks

We were called up this morning. The war is two days old. Now it is afternoon, and we are being held back—even though our forces below are greatly out-numbered. We are being held back until nightfall, when we will have a better chance on the plain; for it is packed with tanks, and we have only two old half-tracks.[2] They are loaded with guns—it is true—but they are lightly armored, they are slow, and they pre-sent high targets. We expect to move at dusk or just before. Then we will descend on the road into the valley and fight amid the shadows. No one wants this: we all are terrified.

The young ones are frightened because, for most of them, this is the first battle. But their fear is not as strong as the blood which is rising and fills their chests with anger and strength. They have little to lose, being, as they are, only eighteen. They look no more fright-ened than members of a sports team before an impor-tant match: it is that kind of fear, for they are respon-sible only to themselves.

Married men, on the other hand, are given away by their eyes and faces. They are saying to themselves, "I must not die; I *must not die.*" They are remembering how they used to feel when they were younger; and they know that they have to fight. They may be killed, but if they don't fight they will surely be killed, be-cause the slow self-made fear which demands constant hesitation is the most efficient of all killers. It is not the cautious who die, but the overcautious. The married men are trying to strike an exact balance between their responsibility as soldiers, their fervent[3] desire to stay alive, and their only hope—which is to go into

---

[2]army vehicles
[3]deeply felt

battle with the smooth, courageous, trancelike movements that will keep them out of trouble. Soldiers who do not know how (like dancers or mountain climbers) to let their bodies think for them are very liable to be killed. There is a flow to hard combat; it is not (as it has often been depicted) entirely chance or entirely skill. A thousand signals and signs speak to you, much as in music. And what a sad moment it is when you must, for one reason or another, ignore them. The married men fear this moment. We should have begun hours ago. Being held back is bad luck.

"What time is it?" asks one of the young soldiers. Someone answers him.

"Fourteen hundred."[4] No one in the Israeli Army except high-ranking officers (colonels, generals—and we have here no colonels or generals) tells time in this fashion.

"What are you, a general?" asks the young soldier. Everyone laughs, as if this were funny, because we are scared. We should not be held back like this.

Another man, a man who is close to fifty and is worrying about his two sons who are in Sinai,[5] keeps on looking at his watch. It is expensive and Japanese, with a black dial. He looks at it every minute to see what time it is, because he has actually forgotten. If he were asked what the time was, he would not be able to respond without checking the watch, even though he has done so fifty times in the last hour. He too is very afraid. The sun glints off the crystal and explodes in our eyes.

As younger men who badly wanted to fight, we thought we knew what courage was. Now we know

---

[4] 2:00 P.M.
[5] site of heavy fighting during the 1960s Arab-Israeli conflicts

that courage is the forced step of going into battle when you want anything in the world but that, when there is every reason to stay out, when you have been through all the tests, and passed them, and think that it's all over. Then the war hits like an artillery shell and you are forced to be eighteen again, but you can't be eighteen again; not with the taste of your wife's mouth in your mouth, not with the smell of her perfume on your wrists. The world turns upside down in minutes.

How hard we struggle in trying to remember the easy courage we once had. But we can't. We must either be brave in a different way, or not at all. What is that way? How can we fight like seasoned[6] soldiers when this morning we kissed our children? There is a way, hidden in the history of war. There must be, for we can see them fighting in the valley; and, high in the air, silver specks are dueling in a dream of blue silence.

Why are we merely watching? To be restrained this way is simply not fair. A quick entrance would get the fear over with, and that would help. But, then again, in the Six Day War, we waited for weeks while the Egyptian Army built up against us. And then, after that torture, we burst out and we leapt across the desert, sprinting, full of energy and fury that kept us like dancers—nimble[7] and absorbed—and kept us alive. That is the secret: You have to be angry. When we arrived on the ridge this morning, we were anything but angry. Now we are beginning to get angry. It is our only salvation. We are angry because we are being held back.

We swear, and kick the sides of the half-tracks. We hate the voice on our radio which keeps telling us to

---

[6]experienced
[7]moving quickly and lightly

hold to our position. We hate that man more than we hate the enemy, for now we want engagement with the enemy. We are beginning to crave battle, and we are getting angrier, and angrier, because we know that by five o'clock we will be worn out. They should let us go now.

A young soldier who has been following the battle, through binoculars, screams. "God!" he says. "Look! Look!"

The Syrians are moving up two columns of armor that will overwhelm our men on the plain below. The sergeant gets on the radio, but from it we hear a sudden waterfall of talk. Holding the microphone in his hand, he listens with us as we discover that they know. They are demanding more air support.

"What air support?" we ask. There is no air-to-ground fighting that we can see. As we watch the Syrians approach, our hearts are full of fear for those of us below. How did our soldiers know? There must be spotters or a patrol somewhere deep in, high on a hill, like us. What air support? There are planes all over the place, but not here.

Then we feel our lungs shaking like drums. The hair on our arms and on the back of our necks stands up and we shake as flights of fighters roar over the hill. They are no more than fifty feet above us. We can feel the heat from the tailpipes, and the orange flames are blinding. The noise is superb. They come three at a time; one wave, two, three, four, five, and six. These are our pilots. The mass of the machinery flying through the air is so great and graceful that we are stunned beyond the noise. We cheer in anger and in satisfaction. It seems the best thing in the world when, as they pass the ridge (How they hug the ground; what superb pilots!) they dip their wings for our sake. They are descending into a thicket of anti-aircraft missiles and radar-directed guns—and they dip their wings for us.

Now we are hot. The married men feel as if rivers are rushing through them, crossing and crashing, for they are angry and full of energy. The sergeant depresses the lever on the microphone. He identifies himself and says, "In the name of God, we want to go in *now.* Damn you if you don't let us go in."

There is hesitation and silence on the other end. "Who is this?" they ask.

"This is Shimon."

More silence, then, "Okay, Shimon. Move! Move!"

The engines start. Now we have our own thunder. It is not even three o'clock. It is the right time; they've caught us at the right time. The soldiers are not slow in mounting the half-tracks. The sound of our roaring engines has magnetized them and they *jump* in. The young drivers race the engines, as they always do.

For a magnificent half minute, we stare into the north light, smiling. The man who tasted the sweet taste of his wife kisses his wrist. The young soldiers are no longer afraid, and the married men are in a perfect sustained[8] fury. Because they love their wives and children, they will not think of them until the battle is over. Now we are soldiers again. The engines are deafening. No longer are we held back. We are shaking; we are crying. Now we stare into the north light, and listen to the explosions below. Now we hear the levers of the gearshifts. Now our drivers exhale and begin to drive. Now we are moving.

---

[8]continual

REFLECT·······························

When were the men "called up" to fight; i.e., brought to the battlefield?

Why are the soldiers being held back from battle? How do they feel about being held back? Why?

Though all the soldiers are frightened, the fears of the married soldiers are different from the fears of the unmarried soldiers. Why?

When do the men finally go into battle? Why does the speaker say, "It is the right time; they've caught us at the right time."

WRITE ·····························

The story describes the effects of fear. Have you ever been really afraid? How did you react? Describe what you were afraid of and how you felt.

Imagine that you are a married soldier waiting for battle. What would you like to say to your wife or husband? To your children? Write a short letter to them, explaining how you feel.

The soldiers in the story are fighting to protect their homeland. What cause—if any—would you fight for? To protect your country? To protect your family? To protect your home or possessions? Explain.

*Randall Jarrell (1914–1965) won a
1961 National Book Award for* The
Woman at the Washington Zoo.

*Do you remember your dreams after you
wake up? As you read, ask yourself, What
did the man dream about? Why won't he
tell his wife?*

The Dream

Randall Jarrell

"What dreams you must have had last night,"
  My wife exclaims with a smile.
"Really, you threshed[1] and muttered
  So loudly, for such a while

"I made up my mind to wake you.
  What was it you were dreaming?"
I yawn and stretch as I answer,
  "I can't remember a thing.

"What did I say?" "Why, nothing—
  I couldn't make out a word.
You whimpered the way a puppy will.
  It was awfully absurd."[2]

I laugh and agree; and all the time
  The thought spins round in my head:
"If you'd guessed why I was crying
  Or what it was I said

"Would you too weep? or speak? or dream
  The dream that troubles me?
Does she know? What would she do?"
  And we smile uncertainly.

---

[1]tossed and turned   [2]silly

REFLECT ·

How did the wife know her husband was dreaming?

Do you think the wife understood anything the husband said in his sleep? Why or why not?

The husband says that he can't remember anything about his dream. Is he telling the truth?

What do you think the husband was dreaming about?

The poem ends with the line "And we smile uncertainly." Explain the feeling between the husband and wife.

WRITE ·

Use one of the following beginnings to write about a dream you have had:

- I recently dreamed that I . . .
- A dream I have often is . . .
- One dream that really upset me was about . . .

The wife asks her husband, "What was it you were dreaming?" Imagine that you are the husband, and write about the dream you had.

The husband in the poem wants to keep his dream private. Where do you go for privacy? Describe a place where you go when you need to be alone.

Billy Morrow Jackson, *Before My Time*, 1964
Union League Club of Chicago

Have you ever had to make sacrifices for
the people you love? If so, you will under-
stand the feelings of Roxie, the woman in
this story. Roxie's way of speaking reflects
where she lives—the rural South. As you
read, notice the details that tell you what
her life has been like. Why does Roxie
want to help other people?

Andrew

Berry Morgan

There was only one time in my life I had a little baby
off all to myself. No kin, that is. I used to love to have
my brother that drives the pulp truck bring *his*, but
Mama couldn't stand too much of their commotion
and they gave her colds with their everlasting sneezes
till we had to wean him from it, and they grew up
hardly ever stopping.

This all began with that white lady that calls me
every year along in the spring to help her set[1] her
ducks. I've fooled with ducks so long now it looks like
they will go on and do anything I want them to, and it
has spread around the country so that I have calls for
it just like a doctor. Well, it's uphill all the way from my
house to this lady's house, and I was taking it nice and
slow and stopping to rest every now and then and look
around. I had got as far as the bluff by the corner of the
old Somerset place and just looked up—I always get
plums from those particular trees since nobody else
seems to know about them—and lo and behold, what

---

[1]aid in the nesting and hatching of eggs

do I see sitting on the gallery[2] of that old tumbled
down cabin but a young girl. Her legs were hanging
loose over the edge and she was swinging them back
and forth and looking down at the road where I was
standing. Do I know her, I thought—because I *do*
know nearly everybody in King County. She might
have come up from Bogue, though, and Mama always
said to stay out of the way of Bogue, white *or* colored,
and I have, but no, if I wasn't telling myself wrong, this
was one of old lady Littell's grandchildren that they've
kept sending her back from Chicago and all around for
years and years.

"Are you all right, honey?" I asked her. "What are
you doing way out here by yourself?"

I was sorry for saying that, because just about
then I saw *him*—or anyhow an undershirt showing up
white at the door. So she must be married, and that
was why she was out here away from school and her
grandmother in this old empty cabin.

"Yes ma'am," she said, taking time to smile with
me and act sweet. "How are you, Miss Roxie?"

So she knew me. Before I could answer, I heard
it—a little high crying noise behind her in the cabin.
Right away I knew what had made it. They had a baby
up in there, their own little baby, and most likely they
were out here tending to it because back in town he
had another rightful wife who would catch him and
get him back. But where was their water, poor things,
what did they do for water? The place didn't have
enough roof left to catch any even if they had a gutter,
which I disbelieved.

The gentleman must have picked it up, because
the crying stopped. I knew I had to some way or other

---

[2]porch

get up on that bluff and hold that little thing myself. "I don't have time right now," I told the girl, "but when I come back from setting a duck could I please see the baby? What is its name?"

She smiled and nodded her head to show manners. "Yes ma'am," she said, "you'd be welcome. Andrew. His name is Andrew."

Well, I went on up the hill to do what I'd said I'd do, and it took nearly all day. This white lady had saved up a winter's talk—wanted to tell me her frights since last spring, has two worrisome boys that she is afraid may drink a little beer. By the time I petted the duck and got it started on its eggs, she had gone on and fixed me a plate of dinner to eat on the back steps so she could talk some more.

The sun was halfway down the woods when I got back to where the cabin was, and reddening up to set because it was March and still cool. I didn't hear anything now except the birds, and I couldn't see any footholds on the outside of the cliff to climb up by. It looked a whole lot different than it had in the morning—long shadows everywhere to make me wonder if they were still up there with it.

It came into my head to give up—Mama always did hate to have me prowling too close to dark. Still I had said I was coming and they might be expecting me. Just then as the good Lord *would* have it, I caught the scent of woodsmoke. So they were still up there and even had themselves a fire. "Hello" I said every once in a while, but my voice doesn't carry and I didn't hear anything back. Just when I got to the top, though, I saw her, standing in the door with a frying pan in her hand—fixing to clean it out, I reckon, because she stooped down to a pile of moss and sticks on the gallery floor.

"How is it?" I asked her. "Is it resting well?"

"Yes ma'am," she said, knocking the frying pan on the gallery edge to clear it. "It seems like it is."

"That's good," I said. "How old is it? How long ago did you find little Andrew?"

I was afraid this had really hurt her feelings, but after a while she told me. "About a week. It's been just about a week." "

"Do you have any milk to nurse it with?"

She shook her head. "It haven't come in yet."

"Well," I said, "that's what I was afraid of. It's got to have its milk, and like Mama used to say, not tomorrow or the next day but right now." I was on the gallery myself by this time, and nearly every board I set my foot on came up at the other end—loose. She tried to watch out for me that I didn't go through until she could push the old door back—it was off its hinges—to make room for me to pass. Right away I saw those foolish children had made a fire in the middle of the floor, just on a piece of roof tin—didn't have sense enough to build it in the fireplace. "Sweet girl," I said, "you're fixing to burn this old place down." And I reached and picked up a piece of rag and took the tin by the corner to pull it onto the hearth.[3] As soon as I straightened up, she took me over to the baby. It was in an old cardboard box, and she had put all the soft things she had under it. It was sound asleep, a precious little boy baby a dark beautiful brown about the same shade, if I reckoned correctly, as Mama. "This is in God's image," I told the girl. "A sign of his love and a brand new life to be used for his glorification. Where's its papa?"

"He's about gone to get milk," the girl answered.

---

[3]fireplace floor

"Leastways that's what I told him to do."

"Does he have any money?"

She bent over the box and looked hard at the baby. Oh, she was proud. You could see that. "He say he have."

I knew Mama wouldn't like me doing this but I couldn't help it. "My house is nice and warm and I have a can of Pet[4] we can put some boiled water with and give it by an eyedropper, just a little at a time until it builds its strength. Come on with me and we will leave *him* a note if you have anything to write on."

She was still smiling all right enough, but she shook her pretty head. "He told me to stay on right here, Miss Roxie, not to leave."

"Is this a King's Town man?"

"No ma'am," she said. "It's a United States soldier."

Just drifting through then, I thought, and apt to drift on. "Well, we've got to give it milk. If you have to wait for the soldier, go ahead and wait, but let me take it on, wrap it in this fresh apron and carry it home. When it's good and strong, you can come and get it."

She leaned over the baby and looked at it again, like it might get up out of its sleep and tell her what to do.

"It's near dark," I said. "You go on and wait if you have to, but I've got to get this baby its supper. And you really ought to go with me and fix yourself up for tomorrow's school—learn something, and not stay out here in these woods with a United States soldier or anybody else." I had wrapped the baby up the best I could, and I kissed its mother and gave her the fifty cents I'd made from setting the duck. Then I was afraid

---

[4] a brand of canned milk

of falling, going down the bluff with it, but by sitting down and sliding on a little at a time I was right down in the road and it was safe.

As soon as I started walking, I began to be happy. This was a real living baby I had to myself—God's image, like I had known it was in the cabin. "If it please Thee," I said, "let this little baby—Andrew is its name—grow strong and tall and take up Thy war against evil." It hardly weighed anything at all.

There is such a change in a house when you first take a baby into it. I put him down on Mama's bed—the first person ever laid there since the evening she passed. "Well sir, Andrew," I said, "there's so much to do and only you and me to do it, I wonder where to start." I could rock it after I put on the water—that would take a while to heat and then cool. By the time I did this, it had its eyes open and was twisting its head a whole lot, like it already knew it had changed its resting place. "Eating is the main thing," I said to it. "After you've had a few drops of weak Pet you'll sleep, and after you sleep I'll strengthen the Pet just enough to make you sleep some more. And all that time you'll be growing and getting bigger. By the time I have to give you back, you'll be looking around here like the Lord of creation—might even have caught on how to smile." If they let me keep him long enough, I could even make him apt[5] in his books, and it made me want to cry to think of him starting to school, getting on the bus and riding off.

Andrew liked rocking. Then after I had given him the first Pet with Mama's eyedropper, I heated a sheet and wrapped his stomach good and rocked some more. He didn't cry at all except when he woke up and

---

[5]smart

wanted more milk. "You are going to keep Roxie up all night," I told him, "but that's all right. When Mama was here, I never was able to sleep more than an hour at a time without her needing something, and now God has sent me a precious lamb in her place."

I would sleep and it would sleep. It felt so good to know it was lying there by me in the dark. I wished it hadn't been given a name yet, because I might name it for Mama's father, the Reverend Isaac Stoner. But you don't hear the name Isaac much anymore and I guess Andrew *was* better.

Along toward morning, even before the mill whistle, I thought I heard a car on our creek road. Who could that be, I thought. They wouldn't come for it before daylight, and besides that the girl and the United States soldier didn't have a car, and whoever this was did. When I heard it drawing up into our yard, I got up and found my wrapper.[6] I braced the baby—it was too little to roll, but still it looked safer with something between it and the edge—and by that time there was knocking on my door.

It was Mr. Bat Becker, the sheriff's helper, and old lady Littell herself, as vexed[7] as she could be.

"I hate to disturb you this time of night," Mr. Bat said, "but there's this little baby missing, and Eliza here's granddaughter says you're the one harboring it."

Well, I took them right in to show them it was safe and happy. But instead of being glad and taking my word, Mrs. Littell, poor old worn-out soul, snatched it off the bed and began looking at every part of it to see if it was true. Then she held it tight and began to moan and cry and kiss it so hard you wouldn't believe she already had a house full of them, all different sizes.

---

[6]shawl
[7]angry

"Mrs. Stoner always did say you were backward,"[8] she told me, "but she didn't let on you were a thief." I felt bad to hear her talk like that, but she was so old and worked up—had been afraid, I guess, that it was thrown back in the woods to buzzards—she couldn't help it. I begged her pardon over and over, and they went on out and slammed the door.

Oh, yes, I see him now and then. Twice I caught up with him at the Piggly[9] and once at the oil station, where they have a Coke machine. And he *is* fine. I give him a nickel if I have one, and he always has a big smile for me—thank you ma'am, no idea in the world who I really am. That's all right, Andrew, I say (just to myself), because I had you for one night, you lying up there in my lap taking milk, and if I'm any judge at all of what is true, you loved me.

---

[8]mentally slow
[9]Piggly Wiggly, a grocery store

REFLECT ·

Who are Andrew's parents?

What made Roxie think that Andrew's mother couldn't take care of him?

Roxie took care of her sick mother. What does this tell you about Roxie?

Mrs. Littell, Andrew's great-grandmother, says that Roxie is "backward." Mrs. Littell also seems to think that Roxie might have hurt the baby. What do you think? Would Roxie make a good mother? Why or why not?

Roxie says she took Andrew to give him food and a warm place to live. But she also seems to have other reasons for wanting Andrew to live with her. What are they?

WRITE ·

Roxie is willing to make sacrifices for the people she loves. Write about a time when you made a sacrifice for someone you love. What did you sacrifice? Why?

What does it take to be a good parent? List and explain the qualities that you believe a person needs to be a good mother or father.

Imagine that Roxie were arrested for kidnapping Andrew. If you were the judge in the case, would you punish Roxie? Describe why you would—or would not—punish her.

When your telephone rings, how do you react? Do you get annoyed, or do you welcome the calls? This poem describes one person's reaction to phone calls and the telephone itself. As you read, ask yourself, Why is the speaker so happy to get phone calls?

The Telephone

Edward Field

My happiness depends on an electric appliance
And I do not mind giving it so much credit
With life in this city being what it is
Each person separated from friends
By a tangle of subways and buses
Yes my telephone is my joy
It tells me that I am in the world and wanted
It rings and I am alerted to love or gossip
I go comb my hair which begins to sparkle
Without it I was like a bear in a cave
Drowsing through a shadowy winter
It rings and spring has come
I stretch and amble[1] out into the sunshine
Hungry again as I pick up the receiver
For the human voice and the good news of friends

---

[1]walk slowly

REFLECT ·

Where does the speaker live? Why has this location made the speaker dependent on the telephone?

What "news" does the speaker get from the telephone calls he receives?

The speaker says that without a telephone, "I was like a bear in a cave / Drowsing through a shadowy winter." Explain the comparison. In what way was the speaker like a bear in the winter?

Do you think the speaker is often lonely? Why or why not?

WRITE ·

When the electric power goes off, which appliance do you miss the most? Radio? TV? CD player? Other? Explain which you miss—and why.

Are you like the speaker, who waits for other people to call? Or are you the one who makes the telephone calls? Explain which kind of person you are.

The speaker of the poem relies on the telephone to communicate with the outside world. Which of the following methods is your favorite way of communicating with friends? Explain why.

- telephone
- letter
- face-to-face conversation

David Park, *Kids on Bikes*, 1950
Courtesy of The Regis Collection, Minneapolis

Raymond Carver (1938–1988) wrote short stories and poems. He won many awards for his writing, including several O. Henry awards.

How do you define manhood? Strength? Maturity? A sense of responsibility toward other people? This story is about a man who wants to be a good father to his son. As you read, think about the men and boys in the story. How do the males show they are "men"?

Bicycles, Muscles, Cigarettes

Raymond Carver

It had been two days since Evan Hamilton had stopped smoking, and it seemed to him everything he'd said and thought for the two days somehow suggested cigarettes. He looked at his hands under the kitchen light. He sniffed his knuckles and his fingers.

"I can smell it," he said.

"I know. It's as if it sweats out of you," Ann Hamilton said. "For three days after I stopped I could smell it on me. Even when I got out of the bath. It was disgusting." She was putting plates on the table for dinner. "I'm so sorry, dear. I know what you're going through. But, if it's any consolation, the second day is always the hardest. The third day is hard, too, of course, but from then on, if you can stay with it that long, you're over the hump. But I'm so happy you're serious about quitting, I can't tell you." She touched his arm. "Now, if you'll just call Roger, we'll eat."

Hamilton opened the front door. It was already

dark. It was early in November and the days were short and cool. An older boy he had never seen before was sitting on a small, well-equipped bicycle in the driveway. The boy leaned forward just off the seat, the toes of his shoes touching the pavement and keeping him upright.

"You Mr. Hamilton?" the boy said.

"Yes, I am," Hamilton said. "What is it? Is it Roger?"

"I guess Roger is down at my house talking to my mother. Kip is there and this boy named Gary Berman. It is about my brother's bike. I don't know for sure," the boy said, twisting the handle grips, "but my mother asked me to come and get you. One of Roger's parents."

"But he's all right?" Hamilton said. "Yes, of course, I'll be right with you."

He went into the house to put his shoes on.

"Did you find him?" Ann Hamilton said.

"He's in some kind of jam," Hamilton answered. "Over a bicycle. Some boy—I didn't catch his name— is outside. He wants one of us to go back with him to his house."

"Is he all right?" Ann Hamilton said and took her apron off.

"Sure, he's all right." Hamilton looked at her and shook his head. "It sounds like it's just a childish argument, and the boy's mother is getting herself involved."

"Do you want me to go?" Ann Hamilton asked.

He thought for a minute. "Yes, I'd rather you went, but I'll go. Just hold dinner until we're back. We shouldn't be long."

"I don't like his being out after dark," Ann Hamilton said. "I don't like it."

The boy was sitting on his bicycle and working the handbrake now.

"How far?" Hamilton said as they started down the sidewalk.

"Over in Arbuckle Court," the boy answered, and when Hamilton looked at him, the boy added, "Not far. About two blocks from here."

"What seems to be the trouble?" Hamilton asked.

"I don't know for sure. I don't understand all of it. He and Kip and this Gary Berman are supposed to have used my brother's bike while we were on vacation, and I guess they wrecked it. On purpose. But I don't know. Anyway, that's what they're talking about. My brother can't find his bike and they had it last, Kip and Roger. My mom is trying to find out where it's at."

"I know Kip," Hamilton said. "Who's this other boy?"

"Gary Berman. I guess he's new in the neighborhood. His dad is coming as soon as he gets home."

They turned a corner. The boy pushed himself along, keeping just slightly ahead. Hamilton saw an orchard, and then they turned another corner onto a dead-end street. He hadn't known of the existence of this street and was sure he would not recognize any of the people who lived here. He looked around him at the unfamiliar houses and was struck with the range of his son's personal life.

The boy turned into a driveway and got off the bicycle and leaned it against the house. When the boy opened the front door, Hamilton followed him through the living room and into the kitchen, where he saw his son sitting on one side of a table along with Kip Hollister and another boy. Hamilton looked closely at Roger and then he turned to the stout, dark-haired woman at the head of the table.

"You're Roger's father?" the woman said to him.

"Yes, my name is Evan Hamilton. Good evening."

"I'm Mrs. Miller, Gilbert's mother," she said. "Sorry to ask you over here, but we have a problem."

Hamilton sat down in a chair at the other end of the table and looked around. A boy of nine or ten, the boy whose bicycle was missing, Hamilton supposed, sat next to the woman. Another boy, fourteen or so, sat on the draining board,[1] legs dangling, and watched another boy who was talking on the telephone. Grinning slyly at something that had just been said to him over the line, the boy reached over to the sink with a cigarette. Hamilton heard the sound of the cigarette sputting out in a glass of water. The boy who had brought him leaned against the refrigerator and crossed his arms.

"Did you get one of Kip's parents?" the woman said to the boy.

"His sister said they were shopping. I went to Gary Berman's and his father will be here in a few minutes. I left the address."

"Mr. Hamilton," the woman said, "I'll tell you what happened. We were on vacation last month and Kip wanted to borrow Gilbert's bike so that Roger could help him with Kip's paper route. I guess Roger's bike had a flat tire or something. Well, as it turns out—"

"Gary was choking me, Dad," Roger said.

"What?" Hamilton said, looking at his son carefully.

"He was choking me. I got the marks." His son pulled down the collar of his T-shirt to show his neck.

"They were out in the garage," the woman con-

---

[1]shelf next to a sink

tinued. "I didn't know what they were doing until Curt, my oldest, went out to see."

"He started it!" Gary Berman said to Hamilton. "He called me a jerk." Gary Berman looked toward the front door.

"I think my bike cost about sixty dollars, you guys," the boy named Gilbert said. "You can pay me for it."

"You keep out of this, Gilbert," the woman said to him.

Hamilton took a breath. "Go on," he said.

"Well, as it turns out, Kip and Roger used Gilbert's bike to help Kip deliver his papers, and then the two of them, and Gary too, they say, took turns rolling it."

"What do you mean 'rolling it'?" Hamilton said.

"Rolling it," the woman said. "Sending it down the street with a push and letting it fall over. Then, mind you—and they just admitted this a few minutes ago—Kip and Roger took it up to the school and threw it against a goalpost."

"Is that true, Roger?" Hamilton said, looking at his son again.

"Part of it's true, Dad," Roger said, looking down and rubbing his finger over the table. "But we only rolled it once. Kip did it, then Gary, and then I did it."

"Once is too much," Hamilton said. "Once is one too many times, Roger. I'm surprised and disappointed in you. And you too, Kip," Hamilton said.

"But you see," the woman said, "someone's fibbing tonight or else not telling all he knows, for the fact is the bike's still missing."

The older boys in the kitchen laughed and kidded with the boy who still talked on the telephone.

"We don't know where the bike is, Mrs. Miller," the boy named Kip said. "We told you already. The last time we saw it was when me and Roger took it to my house after we had it at school. I mean, that was the next to last time. The very last time was when I took it back here the next morning and parked it behind the house." He shook his head. "We don't know where it is," the boy said.

"Sixty dollars," the boy named Gilbert said to the boy named Kip. "You can pay me off like five dollars a week."

"Gilbert, I'm warning you," the woman said. "You see, *they* claim," the woman went on, frowning now, "it disappeared from *here*, from behind the house. But how can we believe them when they haven't been all that truthful this evening?"

"We've told the truth," Roger said. "Everything."

Gilbert leaned back in his chair and shook his head at Hamilton's son.

The doorbell sounded and the boy on the draining board jumped down and went into the living room.

A stiff-shouldered man with a crew haircut and sharp gray eyes entered the kitchen without speaking. He glanced at the woman and moved over behind Gary Berman's chair.

"You must be Mr. Berman?" the woman said. "Happy to meet you. I'm Gilbert's mother, and this is Mr. Hamilton, Roger's father."

The man inclined his head at Hamilton but did not offer his hand.

"What's all this about?" Berman said to his son.

The boys at the table began to speak at once.

"Quiet down!" Berman said. "I'm talking to Gary. You'll get your turn."

The boy began his account of the affair. His father listened closely, now and then narrowing his eyes to study the other two boys.

When Gary Berman had finished, the woman said, "I'd like to get to the bottom of this. I'm not accusing any one of them, you understand, Mr. Hamilton, Mr. Berman—I'd just like to get to the bottom of this." She looked steadily at Roger and Kip, who were shaking their heads at Gary Berman.

"It's not true, Gary," Roger said.

"Dad, can I talk to you in private?" Gary Berman said.

"Let's go," the man said, and they walked into the living room.

Hamilton watched them go. He had the feeling he should stop them, this secrecy. His palms were wet, and he reached to his shirt pocket for a cigarette. Then, breathing deeply, he passed the back of his hand under his nose and said, "Roger, do you know any more about this, other than what you've already said? Do you know where Gilbert's bike is?"

"No, I don't," the boy said. "I swear it."

"When was the last time you saw the bicycle?" Hamilton said.

"When we brought it home from school and left it at Kip's house."

"Kip," Hamilton said, "do you know where Gilbert's bicycle is now?"

"I swear I don't, either," the boy answered. "I brought it back the next morning after we had it at school and I parked it behind the garage."

"I thought you said you left it behind the *house*," the woman said quickly.

"I mean the house! That's what I meant," the boy said.

"Did you come back here some other day to ride it?" she asked, leaning forward.

"No, I didn't," Kip answered.

"Kip?" she said.

"I didn't! I don't know where it is!" the boy shouted.

The woman raised her shoulders and let them drop. "How do you know who or what to believe?" she said to Hamilton. "All I know is, Gilbert's missing a bicycle."

Gary Berman and his father returned to the kitchen.

"It was Roger's idea to roll it," Gary Berman said.

"It was yours!" Roger said, coming out of his chair. "You wanted to! Then you wanted to take it to the orchard and strip it!"

"You shut up!" Berman said to Roger. "You can speak when spoken to, young man, not before. Gary, I'll handle this—dragged out at night because of a couple of roughnecks! Now if either of you," Berman said, looking first at Kip and then Roger, "know where this kid's bicycle is, I'd advise you to start talking."

"I think you're getting out of line," Hamilton said.

"What?" Berman said, his forehead darkening. "And I think you'd do better to mind your own business!"

"Let's go, Roger," Hamilton said, standing up. "Kip, you come now or stay." He turned to the woman. "I don't know what else we can do tonight. I intend to talk this over more with Roger, but if there is a question of restitution[2] I feel since Roger did help manhandle the bike, he can pay a third if it comes to that."

"I don't know what to say," the woman replied, following Hamilton through the living room. "I'll talk to Gilbert's father—he's out of town now. We'll see. It's probably one of those things finally, but I'll talk to his father."

---

[2]paying something back

Hamilton moved to one side so that the boys could pass ahead of him onto the porch, and from behind him he heard Gary Berman say, "He called me a jerk, Dad."

"He did, did he?" Hamilton heard Berman say. "Well, he's the jerk. He looks like a jerk."

Hamilton turned and said, "I think you're seriously out of line here tonight, Mr. Berman. Why don't you get control of yourself?"

"And I told you I think you should keep out of it!" Berman said.

"You get home, Roger," Hamilton said, moistening his lips. "I mean it," he said, "get going!" Roger and Kip moved out to the sidewalk. Hamilton stood in the doorway and looked at Berman, who was crossing the living room with his son.

"Mr. Hamilton," the woman began nervously but did not finish.

"What do you want?" Berman said to him. "Watch out now, get out of my way!" Berman brushed Hamilton's shoulder and Hamilton stepped off the porch into some prickly cracking bushes. He couldn't believe it was happening. He moved out of the bushes and lunged at the man where he stood on the porch. They fell heavily onto the lawn. They rolled on the lawn, Hamilton wrestling Berman onto his back and coming down hard with his knees on the man's biceps. He had Berman by the collar now and began to pound his head against the lawn while the woman cried, "God almighty, someone stop them! For God's sake, someone call the police!"

Hamilton stopped.

Berman looked up at him and said, "Get off me."

"Are you all right?" the woman called to the men as they separated. "For God's sake," she said. She looked at the men, who stood a few feet apart, backs to each other, breathing hard. The older boys had crowded onto the porch to watch; now that it was over, they waited, watching the men, and then they began feinting³ and punching each other on the arms and ribs.

"You boys get back in the house," the woman said. "I never thought I'd see," she said and put her hand on her breast.

Hamilton was sweating and his lungs burned when he tried to take a deep breath. There was a ball of something in his throat so that he couldn't swallow for a minute. He started walking, his son and the boy named Kip at his sides. He heard car doors slam, an engine start. Headlights swept over him as he walked.

Roger sobbed once, and Hamilton put his arm around the boy's shoulders.

"I better get home," Kip said and began to cry. "My dad'll be looking for me," and the boy ran.

"I'm sorry," Hamilton said. "I'm sorry you had to see something like that," Hamilton said to his son.

They kept walking and when they reached their block, Hamilton took his arm away.

"What if he'd picked up a knife, Dad? Or a club?"

"He wouldn't have done anything like that," Hamilton said.

"But what if he had?" his son said.

"It's hard to say what people will do when they're angry," Hamilton said.

They started up the walk to their door. His heart moved when Hamilton saw the lighted windows.

"Let me feel your muscle," his son said.

"Not now," Hamilton said. "You just go in now

---

³pretending to fight

and have your dinner and hurry up to bed. Tell your mother I'm all right and I'm going to sit on the porch for a few minutes."

The boy rocked from one foot to the other and looked at his father, and then he dashed into the house and began calling, "Mom! Mom!"

He sat on the porch and leaned against the garage wall and stretched his legs. The sweat had dried on his forehead. He felt clammy under his clothes.

He had once seen his father—a pale, slow-talking man with slumped shoulders—in something like this. It was a bad one, and both men had been hurt. It had happened in a café. The other man was a farmhand. Hamilton had loved his father and could recall many things about him. But now he recalled his father's one fistfight as if it were all there was to the man.

He was still sitting on the porch when his wife came out.

"Dear God," she said and took his head in her hands. "Come in and shower and then have something to eat and tell me about it. Everything is still warm. Roger has gone to bed."

But he heard his son calling him.

"He's still awake," she said.

"I'll be down in a minute," Hamilton said. "Then maybe we should have a drink."

She shook her head. "I really don't believe any of this yet."

He went into the boy's room and sat down at the foot of the bed.

"It's pretty late and you're still up, so I'll say good night," Hamilton said.

"Good night," the boy said, hands behind his neck, elbows jutting.

He was in his pajamas and had a warm fresh smell

about him that Hamilton breathed deeply. He patted his son through the covers.

"You take it easy from now on. Stay away from that part of the neighborhood, and don't let me ever hear of you damaging a bicycle or any other personal property. Is that clear?" Hamilton said.

The boy nodded. He took his hands from behind his neck and began picking at something on the bedspread.

"Okay, then," Hamilton said, "I'll say good night."

He moved to kiss his son, but the boy began talking.

"Dad, was Grandfather strong like you? When he was your age, I mean, you know, and you—"

"And I was nine years old? Is that what you mean? Yes, I guess he was," Hamilton said.

"Sometimes I can hardly remember him," the boy said. "I don't want to forget him or anything, you know? You know what I mean, Dad?"

When Hamilton did not answer at once, the boy went on. "When you were young, was it like it is with you and me? Did you love him more than me? Or just the same?" The boy said this abruptly. He moved his feet under the covers and looked away. When Hamilton still did not answer, the boy said, "Did he smoke? I think I remember a pipe or something."

"He started smoking a pipe before he died, that's true," Hamilton said. "He used to smoke cigarettes a long time ago and then he'd get depressed with something or other and quit, but later he'd change brands and start in again. Let me show you something," Hamilton said. "Smell the back of my hand."

The boy took the hand in his, sniffed it, and said, "I guess I don't smell anything, Dad. What is it?"

Hamilton sniffed the hand and then the fingers. "Now I can't smell anything, either," he said. "It was there before, but now it's gone." Maybe it was scared out of me, he thought. "I wanted to show you something. All right, it's late now. You better go to sleep," Hamilton said.

The boy rolled onto his side and watched his father walk to the door and watched him put his hand to the switch. And then the boy said, "Dad? You'll think I'm pretty crazy, but I wish I'd known you when you were little. I mean, about as old as I am right now. I don't know how to say it, but I'm lonesome about it. It's like—it's like I miss you already if I think about it now. That's pretty crazy, isn't it? Anyway, please leave the door open."

Hamilton left the door open, and then he thought better of it and closed it halfway.

R EFLECT ·

Why did Roger and Kip borrow Gilbert's bicycle?

How did Roger, Kip, and Gary hurt the bicycle?

In your opinion, which boy or boys are telling the truth about what happened to the bicycle? Which boy or boys are lying? How can you tell?

Why does Mr. Hamilton attack Mr. Berman?

How does Mr. Hamilton feel about the fight he has with Mr. Berman?

How does Roger feel about his father after the fight?

Why does Roger think about his grandfather?

WRITE ·······································

Have you ever been upset by someone's violence? Describe a time when you or someone you know settled an argument with fists instead of reason.

Roger seems both impressed and frightened by his father's behavior. Imagine that you are Roger, and describe how you feel about your father and his fight with Mr. Berman.

After the fight, Mr. Hamilton thinks about his own father and how much they are alike. Which of your parents are you like? Write about the ways in which you are like one of your parents.

Elizabeth Bishop (1911–1979) wrote poems, stories, and nonfiction. In 1956, she won a Pulitzer Prize for her collection of poems North & South: A Cold Spring. *In 1969, she won a National Book Award for* The Complete Poems.

Is there a family-owned store in your neighborhood? In a world of chain stores, it can be nice to find a small business run by people in the neighborhood. This poem is about a gas station that definitely is not part of a chain. Picture what it looks like as you read.

Filling Station

Elizabeth Bishop

Oh, but it is dirty!
—this little filling station,
oil-soaked, oil-permeated[1]
to a disturbing, over-all
black translucency.[2]
Be careful with that match!

Father wears a dirty,
oil-soaked monkey suit[3]
that cuts him under the arms,
and several quick and saucy
and greasy sons assist him
(it's a family filling station),
all quite thoroughly dirty.

---

[1]filled with oil
[2]letting light through but not see-through
[3]mechanic's overalls

Do they live in the station?
It has a cement porch
behind the pumps, and on it
a set of crushed and grease-
impregnated[4] wickerwork;
on the wicker sofa
a dirty dog, quite comfy.

Some comic books provide
the only note of color—
of certain color. They lie
upon a big dim doily
draping a taboret[5]
(part of the set), beside
a big hirsute[6] begonia.[7]

Why the extraneous[8] plant?
Why the taboret?
Why, oh why, the doily?
(Embroidered in daisy stitch
with marguerites,[9] I think,
and heavy with gray crochet.)

Somebody embroidered the doily.
Somebody waters the plant,
or oils it, maybe. Somebody
arranges the rows of cans
so that they softly say:
ESSO[10]—SO—SO—SO
To high-strung automobiles.
Somebody loves us all.

---

[4]filled with grease
[5]low table or stool
[6]hairy
[7]flowering plant

[8]out of place
[9]white flowers with yellow centers
[10]name of an oil company

REFLECT ·

What is the first thing that the speaker notices about the filling station?

Explain why the speaker says, "Be careful with that match!"

Which items show that someone lives at the filling station?

What details in the poem show that someone loves the filling station—and the people in it?

WRITE ·

The speaker finds beauty in an unexpected place. Write about a time when you found beauty where you least expected to find it.

People often personalize an impersonal space by decorating it with items that mean something to them. For example, office workers sometimes decorate their work area with pictures of family members and desk items brought from home. Describe a place that you have "made your own." What items do you keep there? Why are they important to you?

The speaker says that somebody embroidered the doily, waters the plant, and arranges the rows of oil cans. Who do you think that "somebody" is? What is the person like? Describe the person who gives the filling station tender, loving care.

Jacob Lawrence, *Brooklyn Stoop*, 1967
Gouache and casein on paper, 21⅛ × 16⅛ in.
Courtesy of Tacoma Art Museum, Tacoma, Washington
Photograph: Richard Nicol

Can you recall what you thought of adults when you were a child? Older children sometimes think that they "know it all" and that adults are hopelessly out of touch with "real life." Sylvia, the speaker of this story, is one of the know-it-alls. But this streetwise child still has a lot to learn. As you read, think about the title of the story. What lesson is Miss Moore trying to teach Sylvia and the other children?

The Lesson

Toni Cade Bambara

Back in the days when everyone was old and stupid or young and foolish and me and Sugar were the only ones just right, this lady moved on our block with nappy hair and proper speech and no makeup. And quite naturally we laughed at her, laughed the way we did at the junk man who went about his business like he was some big-time president and his sorry-ass horse his secretary. And we kinda hated her too, hated the way we did the winos who cluttered up our parks and pissed on our handball walls and stank up our hall-ways and stairs so you couldn't halfway play hide-and-seek without a goddamn gas mask. Miss Moore was her name. The only woman on the block with no first name. And she was black as hell, cept for her feet, which were fish-white and spooky. And she was always planning these boring-ass things for us to do, us being my cousin, mostly, who lived on the block cause we all moved North the same time and to the same apartment then spread out gradual[1] to breathe. And our parents would yank our heads into some kinda shape and crisp up our clothes so we'd be presentable for travel with Miss Moore, who always looked like she was going to church, though she never did. Which is just one of things the grown-ups talked about when they talked behind her back like a dog. But when she came calling with some sachet[2] she'd sewed up or some gingerbread she'd made or some book, why then they'd all be too embarrassed to turn her down and we'd get handed over all spruced up. She'd been to college and said it was only right that she should take responsibility for the young ones' education, and she not even related by marriage or blood. So they'd go for it. Specially Aunt Gretchen. She was the main gofer in the family. You got some ole dumb shit foolishness you want somebody to go for, you send for Aunt Gretchen. She been screwed into the go-along for so long, it's a blood-deep natural thing with her. Which is how she got saddled with me and Sugar and Junior in the first place while our mothers were in a la-de-da apartment up the block having a good ole time.

So this one day Miss Moore rounds us all up at the mailbox and it's puredee hot and she's knockin herself out about arithmetic. And school suppose to let up in summer I heard, but she don't never let up. And the starch in my pinafore[3] scratching the shit outta me and I'm really hating this nappy-head bitch and her god-damn college degree. I'd much rather go to the pool or to the show where it's cool. So me and Sugar leaning on the mailbox being surly,[4] which is a Miss Moore

---

[1]little by little
[2]a small cloth bag containing perfumed powder
[3]a sleeveless, apron-like dress
[4]in a disagreeable mood

word. And Flyboy checking out what everybody brought for lunch. And Fat Butt already wasting his peanut-butter-and-jelly sandwich like the pig he is. And Junebug punchin on Q.T.'s arm for potato chips. And Rosie Giraffe shifting from one hip to the other waiting for somebody to step on her foot or ask her if she from Georgia so she can kick ass, preferably Mercedes'. And Miss Moore asking us do we know what money is, like we a bunch of retards. I mean real money, she say, like it's only poker chips or monopoly papers we lay on the grocer. So right away I'm tired of this and say so. And would much rather snatch Sugar and go to the Sunset and terrorize the West Indian kids and take their hair ribbons and their money too. And Miss Moore files that remark away for next week's lesson on brotherhood, I can tell. And finally I say we oughta get to the subway cause it's cooler and besides we might meet some cute boys. Sugar done swiped her mama's lipstick, so we ready.

So we heading down the street and she's boring us silly about what things cost and what our parents make and how much goes for rent and how money ain't divided up right in this country. And then she gets to the part about we all poor and live in the slums, which I don't feature.[5] And I'm ready to speak on that, but she steps out in the street and hails two cabs just like that. Then she hustles half the crew in with her and hands me a five-dollar bill and tells me to calculate 10 percent tip for the driver. And we're off. Me and Sugar and Junebug and Flyboy hangin out the window and hollering to everybody, putting lipstick on each other cause Flyboy a faggot anyway, and making farts with our sweaty armpits. But I'm mostly trying to

---

[5]agree with

figure how to spend this money. But they all fascinated
with the meter ticking and Junebug starts laying bets
as to how much it'll read when Flyboy can't hold his
breath no more. Then Sugar lays bets as to how much
it'll be when we get there. So I'm stuck. Don't nobody
want to go for my plan, which is to jump out at the
next light and run off to the first bar-b-que we can
find. Then the driver tells us to get the hell out cause
we there already. And the meter reads eighty-five
cents. And I'm stalling to figure out the tip and Sugar
say give him a dime. And I decide he don't need it bad
as I do, so later for him. But then he tries to take off
with Junebug foot still in the door so we talk about his
mama something ferocious. Then we check out that
we on Fifth Avenue and everybody dressed up in
stockings. One lady in a fur coat, hot as it is. White
folks crazy.

"This is the place," Miss Moore say, presenting it
to us in the voice she uses at the museum. "Let's look
in the windows before we go in."

"Can we steal?" Sugar asks very serious like she's
getting the ground rules squared away before she
plays. "I beg your pardon," say Miss Moore, and we fall
out. So she leads us around the windows of the toy
store and me and Sugar screamin, "This is mine, that's
mine, I gotta have that, that was made for me, I was
born for that," till Big Butt drowns us out.

"Hey, I'm goin to buy that there."

"That there? You don't even know what it is,
stupid."

"I do so," he say punchin on Rosie Giraffe. "It's a
microscope."

"Whatcha gonna do with a microscope, fool?"

"Look at things."

"Like what, Ronald?" ask Miss Moore. And Big Butt
ain't got the first notion. So here go Miss Moore gab-

bing about the thousands of bacteria in a drop of water
and the somethinorother in a speck of blood and the
million and one living things in the air around us is
invisible to the naked eye. And what she say that for?
Junebug go to town on that "naked" and we rolling.
Then Miss Moore ask what it cost. So we all jam into
the window smudgin it up and the price tag say $300.
So then she ask how long'd take for Big Butt and
Junebug to save up their allowances. "Too long," I say.
"Yeh," adds Sugar, "outgrown it by that time." And
Miss Moore say no, you never outgrow learning instruments. "Why, even medical students and interns and,"
blah, blah, blah. And we ready to choke Big Butt for
bringing it up in the first damn place.

"This here costs four hundred eighty dollars," say
Rosie Giraffe. So we pile up all over her to see what
she pointin out. My eyes tell me it's a chunk of glass
cracked with something heavy, and different-color inks
dripped into the splits, then the whole thing put into a
oven or something. But for $480 it don't make sense.

"That's a paperweight made of semi-precious
stones fused[6] together under tremendous pressure,"
she explains slowly, with her hands doing the mining
and all the factory work.

"So what's a paperweight?" asks Rosie Giraffe.

"To weigh paper with, dumbbell," say Flyboy, the
wise man from the East.

"Not exactly," say Miss Moore, which is what she
say when you warm or way off too. "It's to weigh paper
down so it won't scatter and make your desk untidy."
So right away me and Sugar curtsy to each other and
then to Mercedes who is more the tidy type.

"We don't keep paper on top of the desk in my

---

[6]melted

class," say Junebug, figuring Miss Moore crazy or lyin one.

"At home, then," she say. "Don't you have a calendar and a pencil case and a blotter and a letter-opener on your desk at home where you do your homework?" And she know damn well what our homes look like cause she nosys around in them every chance she gets.

"I don't even have a desk," say Junebug. "Do we?"

"No. And I don't get no homework neither," say Big Butt.

"And I don't even have a home," say Flyboy like he do at school to keep the white folks off his back and sorry for him. Send this poor kid to camp posters, is his specialty.

"I do," says Mercedes. "I have a box of stationery on my desk and a picture of my cat. My godmother bought the stationery and the desk. There's a big rose on each sheet and the envelopes smell like roses."

"Who wants to know about your smelly-ass stationery," say Rosie Giraffe fore I can get my two cents in.

"It's important to have a work area all your own so that . . ."

"Will you look at this sailboat, please," say Flyboy, cuttin her off and pointin to the thing like it was his. So once again we tumble all over each other to gaze at this magnificent thing in the toy store which is just big enough to maybe sail two kittens across the pond if you strap them to the posts tight. We all start reciting the price tag like we in assembly. "Handcrafted sailboat of fiberglass at one thousand one hundred ninety-five dollars."

"Unbelievable," I hear myself say and am really stunned. I read it again for myself just in case the group recitation put me in a trance. Same thing. For some reason this pisses me off. We look at Miss Moore and she lookin at us, waiting for I dunno what.

Who'd pay all that when you can buy a sailboat set for a quarter at Pop's, a tube of glue for a dime, and a ball of string for eight cents? "It must have a motor and a whole lot else besides," I say. "My sailboat cost me about fifty cents."

"But will it take water?" say Mercedes with her smart ass.

"Took mine to Alley Pond Park once," say Flyboy. "String broke. Lost it. Pity."

"Sailed mine in Central Park and it keeled over and sank. Had to ask my father for another dollar."

"And you got the strap," laugh Big Butt. "The jerk didn't even have a string on it. My old man wailed[7] on his behind."

Little Q.T. was staring hard at the sailboat and you could see he wanted it bad. But he too little and somebody'd just take it from him. So what the hell. "This boat for kids, Miss Moore?"

"Parents silly to buy something like that just to get all broke up," say Rosie Giraffe.

"That much money it should last forever," I figure.

"My father'd buy it for me if I wanted it."

"Your father, my ass," say Rosie Giraffe getting a chance to finally push Mercedes.

"Must be rich people shop here," say Q.T.

"You are a very bright boy," say Flyboy. "What was your first clue?" And he rap him on the head with the back of his knuckles, since Q.T. the only one he could get away with. Though Q.T. liable[8] to come up behind you years later and get his licks in when you half expect it.

---

[7]whipped
[8]is likely to

"What I want to know is," I says to Miss Moore though I never talk to her, I wouldn't give the bitch that satisfaction, "is how much a real boat costs? I figure a thousand'd get you a yacht any day."

"Why don't you check that out," she says, "and report back to the group?" Which really pains my ass. If you gonna mess up a perfectly good swim day least you could do is have some answers. "Let's go in," she say like she got something up her sleeve. Only she don't lead the way. So me and Sugar turn the corner to where the entrance is, but when we get there I kinda hang back. Not that I'm scared, what's there to be afraid of, just a toy store. But I feel funny, shame. But what I got to be shamed about? Got as much right to go in as anybody. But somehow I can't seem to get hold of the door, so I step away for Sugar to lead. But she hangs back too. And I look at her and she looks at me and this is ridiculous. I mean, damn, I have never ever been shy about doing nothing or going nowhere. But then Mercedes steps up and then Rosie Giraffe and Big Butt crowd in behind and shove, and next thing we all stuffed into the doorway with only Mercedes squeezing past us, smoothing out her jumper and walking right down the aisle. Then the rest of us tumble in like a glued-together jigsaw done all wrong. And people lookin at us. And it's like the time me and Sugar crashed into the Catholic church on a dare. But once we got in there and everything so hushed and holy and the candles and the bowin and the handkerchiefs on all the drooping heads, I just couldn't go through with the plan. Which was for me to run up to the altar and do a tap dance while Sugar played the nose flute and messed around in the holy water. And Sugar kept givin me the elbow. Then later teased me so bad I tied her up in the shower and turned it on and locked her in. And she'd be there till this day if Aunt Gretchen hadn't finally figured I was lyin about the boarder takin a shower.

Same thing in the store. We all walkin on tiptoe and hardly touchin the games and puzzles and things. And I watched Miss Moore who is steady watchin us like she waitin for a sign. Like Mama Drewery watches the sky and sniffs the air and takes note of just how much slant is in the bird formation. Then me and Sugar bump smack into each other, so busy gazing at the toys, 'specially the sailboat. But we don't laugh and go into our fat-lady bump-stomach routine. We just stare at that price tag. Then Sugar run a finger over the whole boat. And I'm jealous and want to hit her. Maybe not her, but I sure want to punch somebody in the mouth.

"Watcha bring us here for, Miss Moore?"

"You sound angry, Sylvia. Are you mad about something?" Givin me one of them grins like she tellin a grown-up joke that never turns out to be funny. And she's lookin very closely at me like maybe she plannin to do my portrait from memory. I'm mad, but I won't give her that satisfaction. So I slouch around the store bein very bored and say, "Let's go."

Me and Sugar at the back of the train watchin the tracks whizzin by large then small then gettin gobbled up in the dark. I'm thinkin about this tricky toy I saw in the store. A clown that somersaults on a bar then does chin-ups just cause you yank lightly at his leg. Cost $35. I could see me askin my mother for a $35 birthday clown. "You wanna who that costs what?" she'd say, cocking her head to the side to get a better view of the hole in my head. Thirty-five dollars could buy new bunk beds for Junior and Gretchen's boy. Thirty-five dollars and the whole household could go visit Granddaddy Nelson in the country. Thirty-five dollars would pay for the rent and the piano bill too.

Who are these people that spend that much for per-
forming clowns and $1,000 for toy sailboats? What
kinda work they do and how they live and how come
we ain't in on it? Where we are is who we are, Miss
Moore always pointin out. But it don't necessarily have
to be that way, she always adds then waits for somebody to say that poor people have to wake up and
demand their share of the pie and don't none of us
know what kind of pie she talkin about in the first
damn place. But she ain't so smart cause I still got her
four dollars from the taxi and she sure ain't gettin it.
Messin up my day with this shit. Sugar nudges me in
my pocket and winks.

Miss Moore lines us up in front of the mailbox
where we started from, seem like years ago, and I got
a headache for thinkin so hard. And we lean all over
each other so we can hold up under the draggy-ass
lecture she always finishes us off with at the end before we thank her for borin us to tears. But she just
looks at us like she readin tea leaves. Finally she say,
"Well, what did you think of F.A.O. Schwarz?"[9]

Rosie Giraffe mumbles, "White folks crazy."

"I'd like to go there again when I get my birthday
money," says Mercedes, and we shove her out the pack
so she has to lean on the mailbox by herself.

"I'd like a shower. Tiring day," say Flyboy.

Then Sugar surprises me by sayin, "You know,
Miss Moore, I don't think all of us here put together eat
in a year what that sailboat costs." And Miss Moore
lights up like somebody goosed her. "And?" she say,
urging Sugar on. Only I'm standin on her foot so she
don't continue.

"Imagine for a minute what kind of society it is in

---

[9]a large toy store in New York City

which some people can spend on a toy what it would cost to feed a family of six or seven. What do you think?"

"I think," say Sugar pushing me off her feet like she never done before, cause I whip her ass in a minute, "that this is not much of a democracy if you ask me. Equal chance to pursue happiness means an equal crack at the dough, don't it?" Miss Moore is besides herself and I am disgusted with Sugar's treachery. So I stand on her foot one more time to see if she'll shove me. She shuts up, and Miss Moore looks at me, sorrowfully I'm thinkin. And somethin weird is goin on, I can feel it in my chest.

"Anybody else learn anything today?" lookin dead at me. I walk away and Sugar has to run to catch up and don't even seem to notice when I shrug her arm off my shoulder.

"Well, we got four dollars anyway," she says.

"Uh hunh."

"We could go to Hascombs and get half a chocolate layer and then go to the Sunset and still have plenty money for potato chips and ice-cream sodas."

"Uh hunh."

"Race you to Hascombs," she say.

We start down the block and she gets ahead which is O.K. by me cause I'm goin to the West End and then over to the Drive to think this day through. She can run if she want to and even run faster. But ain't nobody gonna beat me at nuthin.

REFLECT ·······························

Where do the children live? Describe their neighborhood.

How does Sylvia feel about Miss Moore? Why?

What items do the children see in the toy store
window? How much does each cost?

How do Sylvia and Sugar feel when they first enter
the toy store?

Describe the lesson that Miss Moore is trying to teach
the children.

Does Sylvia learn the lesson? How do you know?

The writer of the story has Sylvia use "bad grammar"
and swearwords. Why? Would it improve the story if
Sylvia spoke differently? Why or why not?

WRITE ·······························

Describe a lesson in life that you learned when you
were a child.

The story takes place in two settings—a poor
neighborhood and a rich neighborhood. Write about
two different neighborhoods in your town or city.
Describe what each looks like and how the two
neighborhoods are different.

"The Lesson" is told from Sylvia's point of view. Miss
Moore's viewpoint is very different. Imagine that you
are Miss Moore. Write a page in your diary or journal
about your trip to the toy store. Explain why you
took the children, how they reacted, and what you
hope they learned.

CREDITS

Poem on pages 1-2: "They Went Home," from *Just Give Me a Cool Drink of Water . . . 'Fore I Diiie*, by Maya Angelou. Copyright © 1971 by Maya Angelou. Reprinted by permission of Random House, Inc.

Story on pages 5-7: "Early Autumn," from *Something in Common and Other Stories*, by Langston Hughes. Copyright © 1963 by Langston Hughes. Reprinted by permission of Hill and Wang, a division of Farrar, Straus and Giroux, Inc.

Poem on pages 10-11: "The Sunday News," reprinted from *Daily Horoscope*, by Dana Gioia (Graywolf Press, 1986). Reprinted with the permission of Graywolf Press.

Story on pages 13-20: "One Throw" by W. C. Heinz, from *The Fireside Book of Baseball*, 1950 edition. Copyright © 1950 by W. C. Heinz, renewed 1978. Reprinted by permission of William Morris Agency, Inc., on behalf of the author.

Poem on pages 22-23: "APO 96225," by Larry Rottmann, from *Carrying the Darkness*, edited by W. D. Ehrhard. Reprinted with permission of author.

Story on pages 27-31: "Tickits," by Paul Milenski. Published in the *Available Press/PEN Short Story Collection* (New York: Ballantine, 1985), in cooperation with the PEN Syndicated Fiction Project. Reprinted by permission of the Project.

Poem on pages 32-33: "Collect Calls," by Diana Bickston, from *The Light from Another Country*, edited by Joseph Bruchac (Greenfield Center, NY: The Greenfield Review Press, 1984). Reprinted with permission of the editor.

Story on pages 35-40: "Speed Cleen," by James Stevenson. Reprinted by permission: Copyright © 1968, The New Yorker Magazine, Inc.

Poem on page 42: "Montgomery," by Sam Cornish, from *Natural Process*, edited by Ted Wilentz and Tom Weatherly. Copyright © 1970 by Hill and Wang, Inc. Reprinted by permission of Hill and Wang, a division of Farrar, Straus and Giroux, Inc.

Story on pages 45-53: "She Said a Bad Word," by Jose Yglesias. Published in the *Available Press/PEN Short Story Collection* (New York: Ballantine, 1985), in cooperation with the PEN Syndicated Fiction Project. Reprinted by permission of the Project.

Poem on pages 55-56: "Note to the Previous Tenants," from *Tossing and Turning*, by John Updike. Copyright © 1977 by John Updike. Reprinted by permission of Alfred A. Knopf, Inc.